Foreword

I grew up in my mother's kitchen, where an endless stream of hungry friends would pass through, lifting pot lids and sniffing the contents with delight. We were the only Indian family where you never really knew which new dish would be made on any particular day. We ate all types of eastern cuisine, experimented with paellas and pavlova, roasted chickens and ducks in orange sauce and made soufflé. Mom's green bean and potato curry is legendary. Meals were prepared at a minutes notice as guests arrived invariably at dinner time and would be invited to stay for a meal. We were lucky enough to always have fresh herbs a hand's reach away, and a well-stocked cupboard of essential staples that made it easy to whip something delicious into being.

My mom is a master at making a plan. She's able to make magic with a few breadcrumbs and some seasoning, add potatoes and you have an entrée. It has been an enormous privilege to learn how to cook under the watch of someone so easy about the learning process. She's taken all of her phone cooking tutorial expertise (Mom help! How do you make…?) and poured it along with a generous dose of her love for beautiful food into this book. This is my mom's vegetarian kitchen, in one amazing book. May you have many beautiful meals with the people you love, like we have, savouring the food made from these awesome recipes.

Fiona Juan

"No one who cooks, cooks alone. Even at her most solitary, a cook in the kitchen is surrounded by generations of cooks past, the advice and menus of cooks present, the wisdom of cookbook writers."
— Laurie Colwin

Table of Contents

BHENGORI'S VEGETARIAN COOKBOOK

Wholesome Vegetarian Cooking for a busy Lifestyle

Rashida Dawood Juan

ISBN: 1515292711
ISBN-13: 978-1515292715

DEDICATION

To all my children and their friends who stayed with us, tested my cooking and encouraged me to compile this book of recipes.

Understanding some Terms

BASTE: To moisten food with marinade, butter or pan juices during cooking frying or roasting. Basting prevents drying and adds to the flavour.

BEURRE MAINE: French cooking term for kneaded butter, a mixture of softened butter and flour are kneaded together to use to thicken soups sauces and stews. To prepare: combine25g butter and 25g flour in a bowl. Knead the mixture and shape into balls and refrigerate. Use required.

BIND: To use beaten egg or a sauce to hold other ingredients together. Vegetarians use flour chick pea flour or any other non-animal derived 'sticky' substance to 'bind' ingredients together.

BLANCH: To briefly heat foods in a large quantity of boiling water.

BOIL: To heat the liquid until bubbles form rapidly on the surface.

BOUQUET GARNI: A bunch of different herbs tied together with a string or secured in a muslin bag. It is used to flavour soups, stews, and foods during cooking and then discarded before the dish is served.

BRAISE: To sear meat over high heat in oil or fat and then cook on low heat. Some vegetables are also treated this way to seal the juice e.g. Brinjal and okra.

CARAMALISE: To heat sugar until it forms a golden brown syrup or to coat a mould or food with caramel.

COURT BOUILLON OR STOCK: A liquid used for poaching fish or vegetables to give extra flavour. A basic stock or bouillon can be prepared by boiling 2 carrots, 2 onions, a celery stick and a bouquet garnish in salted water for at least 20min.The liquid is the stock.

CROUTONS: Small cubes of bread that have been toasted in a 150 ° oven for 5 minutes, then tossed with melted butter or oil. Another way to make croutons is to fry bread cubes in hot oil till golden brown.

DE GLAZE: To scrape juices and brown particles from a utensil used for roasting by adding water stock or wine. When a small quantity of flour mixed with water is briskly stirred into the liquid and heated, simple gravy is formed.

DREDGE: To sprinkle foods lightly with flour or sugar to coat.

GARNISH: To decorate a dish just before serving with colourful extras e.g. Parsley, watercress, croutons, lemon, tomatoes and coriander.

GLAZE: (a) To put a dish under the grill to form a golden brown crust before serving.
(b) To coat with an icing or sugar syrup when preparing bread, pastries cakes and pies.

MARINATE: To soak food in a liquid (the marinade), to season and tenderise before cooking. A marinade is made of oil and vinegar, or lemon juice or wine and appropriate spices and seasonings for the dish.

REDUCE: To decrease the amount of liquid by boiling uncovered, over high heat. Reducing is done to intensify the flavour and to improve the consistency of the liquid.

REFRESH: To stop the cooking process by immediately plunging cooked foods into cold water. Refreshing helps to retain flavour and sets colour.

ROUX: A mixture of butter and flour, cooked gently over low heat .Used to thicken sauces and soups or the base of a variety of white and brown sauces.

SAUTÉ: To fry quickly in a small amount of oil or fat.

SHRED: To cut or pull apart meat or vegetables into thin strips.

SIMMER: To cook foods in a liquid heated to just below boiling point. When simmering and the liquid begins to boil, lower the cooking temperature.

SLIVER: To chop food, especially nuts, into thin strips.

STEAM: To cook meat fish or vegetables or puddings in a covered pan placed over boiling water. The food is cooked by the intense steam given off by the water.

VINAIGRETTE: A basic salad dressing consisting of 3 parts oil to 1 part vinegar.

PRE-SOAK: Pre-soak overnight. Most dried beans and lentils can be covered with boiling water and allowed to stand overnight. This process rehydrates the foods and lessens the cooking time as well as helps save fuel.

MAKE A PASTE: Adding a little water to spices to make a paste prevents spices from burning or changing colour when added to hot oil.

BROWN SPICES: These are spices like cinnamon, cloves, cardamom, mustard seeds and cumin seeds. These, when added to oil when oil is heating, release their flavour into the oil making food more fragrant.

Conversion Table

CUP CONVERSIONS	CUPS AND SPOON	
1cup cake or bread flour 136g	1 cup 250ml	
1 cup nutty wheat flour 124g	½ cup 125ml	
1 cup corn four 146g	¼ cup 62ml	
1 cup white sugar 202g	1 tsp 5ml	
1 cup castor sugar 218g	1 dessert spoon 10ml	
1 cup light brown sugar 216g	1 tbsp 15ml	
1 cup dark brown sugar	150g	
1 cup butter	250g	
1 cup nuts	105g	
1 cup dried fruit	190g	
1 cup raisins	190g	
1 cup desiccated coconut	78g	
1 cup cocoa	80g	
1 cup digestive bran	40g	
1 cup fresh bread crumbs	50g	
1 cup honey or syrup	360g	
1 cup uncooked rice	186g	

Weights

1kg	1000g	2.2lb
100g		3 and $^{1}/_{4}$oz
1lb		450g
1oz		30g

Liquid Measurements

1 litre	1 and $^{3}/_{4}$pints	53fl oz
1 pint	570ml	120fl oz
1 fl oz	30ml	

Measurements

A 10g sachet of Instant yeast is equal to 15ml (1 tablespoon) of fresh yeast which comes in 25g cubes.

25g fresh yeast = 10g dry yeast

Oven Temperatures

	CELCIUS (^{0}C)	FAHRENHEIT	GASMARK
Very Slow	120	250	1
Slow	150	300	1
Moderately Slow	160	325	3
Moderate	180	350	4
Moderately Hot	190	375	5
Hot	200	400	6
Very Hot	320	450	7

Spices

> "Tomatoes and oregano make it Italian; wine and tarragon make it French. Sour cream makes it Russian; lemon and cinnamon make it Greek. Soy sauce makes it Chinese; garlic makes it good."
> — Alice May Brock

Ginger and Garlic

Most Indian vegetarian dishes include both ginger and garlic. However there are some religions that forbid the use of garlic and some root vegetables like onions. These vegetables cannot be consumed in any form. Where onions have to be sautéed yellow asafetida can be substituted: ½ teaspoon of the powder can be substituted per ½ cup chopped onions. Omit the garlic and the recipe can be used.
Ginger and garlic can be purchased from the vegetable section of the super market. Some shops also keep containers of ginger and garlic combinations. Be sure to open the container and smell the garlic before purchasing. There has to be a strong smell of garlic to determine its freshness.

Use of spices:

The secret of success with spices is the understanding of their uses. Brown spices are used mostly for their aroma. In order to extract maximum benefit from these spices cardamom, clove, cinnamon, mustard seeds are added to the cooking oil when onions are sautéed. The hot oil extracts most of the flavour and aroma from the spices.
Turmeric powder, chilli powder, and saffron add colour.
Other spices add flavour and taste.
Curry leaves are added into the dish while it is cooking. Thyme, rosemary, lemon grass, oregano are added into the food, while cooking.
Coriander leaves, parsley and chives are used in stir fries, or added as garnishes.
Some herbs e.g. Sweet basil and mint are added before serving.
Remember that without the sense of smell one cannot taste. Therefore both taste and smell go hand in hand.
My neighbours' tell me that they can almost taste the food in the street as they pass my house.
Spices are normally added to hot oil. Be sure to add a little water to the spices and make a paste of the spices before adding to the oil. When spices are added to hot oil, they burn instead of cooking. This is why the colour of the spices changes when added to hot oil. Burnt spices change the taste of the dish making it bitter.

Beans and Lentils:

To save on cooking time soak beans and lentils overnight if possible.

Dried soy chunks and mince:
Dried soy mince and chunks mince have to be soaked for a few hours before washing and cooking. These have to be thoroughly washed and rinsed. Sometimes spicing them overnight enhances the taste.

Handy Hints

*"I like a cook who smiles out loud when he tastes his own work.
Let God worry about your modesty; I want to see your enthusiasm."*
— Robert Farrar Capon

The Cooking crock or Slow Cooker: I found this pot to be very useful for the working person. It is time consuming cooking beans and lentils .For those beans and lentils that take several hours to boil, simply soak in hot water overnight. In the morning, prepare in the usual way and allow to simmer for five minutes. Then pour the contents into your Slow Cooker and set the temperature on low if you need the food for the evening. Make sure that the level of the water just covers the beans. Cover the pot and go to work. You will be greeted with the aroma of freshly cooked food when you enter your home. Similarly, if you want the meal for the morning, soak the beans in the morning .Then prepare and allow it to cook at night. You will be greeted with the aroma of food in the morning. This is one pot you don't have to watch.

Non-stick pans are ideal for today's health conscious cooks. Use these to create meals using less oil. Washing these pots and pans is also easier. Fry courgettes and eggplant or aubergines in one tablespoon of olive oil in a non-stick frying pan.

Pasta made of semolina has more fibre.

When making Gnocchi use potato and whole-wheat flour.

Lentils have more fibre and leave you fuller for longer.

Make your own tomato sauce by simmering tomatoes over low heat. Add a teaspoon of sugar in 500gm of tomatoes to take away the tartness.

Coconut milk is very fattening. Substitute by using a teaspoon of coconut essence into a tin of Ideal milk, or buy low fat.

Substitute wheat flour for bean flour, potato flour or oats 1 to 1 when baking.

If a recipe asks for 2 cups of oil substitute with only 80 ml of oil .Add skim milk to make up for the liquid.

Substitute sweet potato or pumpkin for fats and oils in recipes.

Use grape seed oil or macadamia oil or olive oil for other oil.

Use 2 blocks of melted chocolate to ice a cake instead of conventional icing sugar.

Use yogurt and fat free cottage cheese instead of cream.

Use 30 gm low fat cheese per 100 of cheese required.

Sprinkle cheese on top of food instead of into it. Use Parmesan cheese which has a strong flavour so less can be used.

Use fat free cottage cheese and yogurt to make cheese cake.

Some brown bread is coloured with caramel so it is better to use wholegrain bread. Eat less and eat slowly.

A few grains of fenugreek seeds added to lentils and beans relieve the flatulence problem.

> "Vegetables are a must on a diet. I suggest carrot cake, zucchini bread, and pumpkin pie."
> Jim Davis

Lowering Cholesterol:
The following foods have to be included in the diet to lower cholesterol.
All Bran Flakes
Oat meal
Dried Fruit
Whole wheat and whole wheat products
Baked potato with skin
Green leafy vegetables
Nuts
Bananas

My Store Cupboard:
Green moong and moong dhall.
Chick peas and gram dhall.
Brown lentils (masoor) and masoor dhall.
Dried peas and split peas (pea dhall).
Large brown lentils.
Sugar beans and large white beans.
Cow peas.
Brown rice, sushi, Basmati, Aborio, American long grain and wild rice.
Soya chunks and soya mince (dry).
Dry onion flakes and dry garlic flakes.

Canned vegetables:
All types of beans.
Whole peeled tomatoes.
Chopped tomatoes.
Tomato and onion mix.
Tomato puree in tins and individual sachets.
Peas.
Sweet corn (cream style and whole kernel).

Frozen vegetables:
Beans, Peas, mixed vegetables, stir-fry vegetables, cauliflower, broccoli, Brussels' sprouts etc.
NB! When buying any processed products, be sure to read the labels. Depending on the brand, they may or may not be suited for pure vegetarian diets.

FRYS products: (processed soya products).
Hot dogs, sausages, burger patties, soya mince, soya strips, soya polony, and vegetable patties.

Quorn products :
Quorn is made with mycoprotein and are a good alternative to soya. They come in the same meat analogue formats that most soy products have eg. Mince, strips etc.

Other soya products:
Soya prawns, soya chicken strips, soya steaks etc.

Other Groceries

Condensed milk condensed cream Nespray milk powder
Custard powder NO egg (egg substitute) baking powder
Bicarbonate of soda, vegetarian jellies, vegetarian Gelatine
Egg free mayonnaise. Soya powder potato powder
Polenta mealie meal, cous cous
Ground rice flour, semolina coconut milk
Maizena flour(cake and bread)pasta
Sugar, honey, sour milk (maas)
Yogurt, fresh milk, butter
Ghee, olive oil, Vegetable oil vegan margarine Vegan spread, Salt

Some ingredient substitutes and where to find them

For various reasons some products cannot be used in a particular recipe. These are a few substitutes that I have found to work well.

PRODUCT	WHERE FOUND
Jellozone: Vegetable Gelatine	Health shops
Egg Replacer: An Ogram product from Australia called No Eggs. Is an excellent natural egg replacer and can be used for baking, Fillings, batter and custards. 1 pack equals to 66 eggs	Found at most supermarkets and health shops
Spray and Cook: Contains lecithin which is an odourless, natural soya bean extract. South African product that is both ozone friendly and cholesterol free	Found in most super markets
Carob Powder: Great tasting chocolate substitute	Found in most Health Stores and Pharmacies
Nespray milk powder	In most super markets on the milk powder shelves
Mayonnaise: Called From Mommy with Love Egg free, cholesterol free and no added colorants and preservatives. Same name salad dressing also available	Found Checkers. Made in Cape Town
Stork Cremendous: A savoury and dessert topping which contains Vegetable Fats ,buttermilk, emulcifiers (including Soya lecithin) ,stabilizers and colourants. Contains no preservatives and is also halaal	Found in most super markets
Natures Choice Herbal Salt: Is an aluminium free, iodine free Sea salt and herb mix	Found in most health shops
No Salt: Natures Choice (potassium chloride) for low sodium diet	Found in most health shops
Rossmoor: Gelatine powder (halaal) Quick dissolving and unflavoured	Found in Indian grocery shops a product of Pakistan

Time saving hints for the busy cook:
The modern kitchen comes well equipped for easy food preparation but one must consider appliances that assist in making ones work easy and less time consuming.
Invest in good stainless steel cooking pots,
Non-stick pots and sauce pans.
Not stick frying pans,
Silicone baking pans, and trays,
Good knives, chopping boards,
Wooden spoons or silicone spoons,
Whisk, spatulas, and lifting spoons.
Measuring cups and spoons, and mixing bowls.

Appliances:
Food Processor, Blender, Smoothie maker, Coffee or Spice grinder, Slow cooker

Other Useful Kitchen Tools
Colander, sieve, mortar and pestle and rolling pin

Useful Ingredients

1. Arrowroot:
This is a thickening agent for soups and puddings. It is tasteless and becomes clear when cooked. It is found in Asian food stores and natural food and health shops. It is used as corn starch or in place of eggs in quiches.

2. Basmati Rice:
This rice is used traditionally used in Indian and Middle Eastern cuisines. It is the most easily digestible long grain rice. It is available in most super markets and Asian food stores.

3. Bean Sprouts:
These are usually used in Asian foods. The crisp sprouts of mung beans and other lentils can be enjoyed in salads and sandwiches .These are found in supermarkets in the vegetable section. You can also make your own. They are rich in vitamins and minerals and considered as one of the few <complete> foods.

4. Buck Wheat:
It has a light bland flavour and is considered similar to cereal such as oats barley or wheat. It usually comes in the form of sprouts and has a mild flavour like lettuce. Buck wheat flour is used sometimes in pan cakes and muffins. It is also used in breads salads and cakes.

5. Bulgur Wheat:
It is parboiled wheat which is used in place of rice in the Middle East. It has a nutty flavour. It is found in super markets and natural food stores.

6. Capers:
This has a sharp vinegary flavour and is used in salads. Capers should be drained and rinsed before using. Capers are found in most super markets.

7. Celery Salt:
This is a pungent mixture of fine grained salt and ground celery seed. It is a seasoning used to sprinkle on vegetables, salads and vegetable juices.

8. Chilli Paste:
This is made from a number of ingredients: garlic, hot chilli peppers, and vinegar are pounded together to flavour and add kick to recipes; especially stir fries. This paste can be found in most Asian shops.

9. Chives:
This is a member of the onion family. Shallot leaves can be used in place of chives. These long stalks can be cut fine and frozen in plastic bags. As chives are used as a garnish they are used last when cooking.

10. Chutney:
It is made with a combination of fruit and vegetables.-can be very sweet and sour or a variation of sweet and sour and spicy. One can buy it at a super market or make it at home.

11. Cider Vinegar:
Add a lovely fruity flavour to recipes by using this vinegar. It is milder and sweeter than other vinegars and can be found in most super markets.

12. Balsamic Vinegar:
This is strongly flavoured. It is a sweet red wine vinegar, available in most super markets. Use less than other vinegars.

13. Cilantro or Coriander;(dhaniya):
Fresh leaves and seeds are used in Indian Asian and Mexican cooking.

14. Cloves:
Cloves are the unopened buds of myrtle flowers. Can be found whole or ground. It is used in Eastern cuisines. It is found in most super markets and Asian shops.

4. White Balsamic vinegar and red balsamic vinegar are made from the same grapes except that a different process is used to lighten the white vinegar. Dark balsamic is used in sauces, pasta, salads deserts and to deglaze a pan.

5. Rice vinegar is made from rice wine. It has a slightly sweet flavour and is especially good with raw vegetable salad .It is also used for marinating and preparing Chinese or Japanese dishes.

6. Flavoured vinegars: are prepared by flavouring with herbs, spices, flowers, fruit and vegetables. These are used for sauces and dressings.

FRIED BHINDI

How to make your own

YOGURT
Ingredients:
2 ½ cups milk
¼ cup full cream milk powder
2 tbsp plain yogurt - for the culture
Method:
1. Combine milk and powdered milk and mix until smooth.
2. Pour into sauce pan and bring to boil while stirring. Remove from the heat and cool to lukewarm. (50°C)
3. Place yogurt in a bowl and gradually add in warm milk. The liquid should be lukewarm. Strain the liquid.
4. Pour mixture into a clean glass jar and keep in a warm place, without moving it for 24 hrs. Refrigerate before using.

SOY MILK
Ingredients:
1 cup soy milk powder
1 litre water

Mix and use or:
$^2/_3$ cup dried soya beans boiled in 1 litre water and strained

Method:
1. Soak beans by pouring boiling water to cover them. Allow to stand overnight.
2. Rinse beans and rub skin with the tips of your fingers to remove skins from the beans. Discard skins.
3. Blend and process beans until they are finely ground.
4. Spoon mixture into a bag made of muslin cloth. Place bag into a large bowl. Cover with water.
5. Allow water to fill bag. Squeeze several times to remove juice. The bag serves as a sieve.
6. 1 litre makes 4 cups.

COTTAGE CHEESE
Ingredients:
2 litres of milk
2 tbsp sour cream
Method:
1 Heat milk in a large sauce pan until milk is luke-warm. Place sour cream in a bowl, add warm milk stirring gradually all the milk. Cover, and let it stand at room temperature for 48 hours or until the mixture is thick. If the weather is hot the mixture will take 24hrs to thicken.
2. Drop a piece of muslin cloth into a pan of boiling water to sterilise, remove and wring out the cloth. Spread out over the top of a large bowl. Pour the curd into the bowl. Gather the corners of the cloth and secure with string. Suspend with string over a basin to drain.
3. Remove from cloth and refrigerate before using.

PANEER

This is made in the same way but the bundle of cheese is not removed from the cloth. It is weighed down by placing something heavy on it to act as a press to harden it. This takes 24 hrs. When it is hardened it can be cut into cubes and refrigerated.

PEANUT BUTTER

Ingredients:
250g. Shelled roasted unsalted peanuts.
2 tbsp cooking oil

Method:
1. Combine all ingredients in a blender or processor. Blend until smooth as desired.

SELF RAISING FLOUR

Ingredients:
2 cups flour
2 tsp baking powder

Method:
Sift flour and baking powder together

BAKING POWDER

Ingredients:
1 level tsp cream of Tatar
½ level tsp bicarbonate of soda

Method:
1. Blend the above ingredients to make 2 tsps of baking powder.
2. Baking powder is a rising agent made up of combining an acid and an alkali together.

COCONUT MILK

Coconut milk is not the liquid inside the coconut. It is made.

Ingredients:
2 cups desiccated coconut
2½ cups hot water

Method:
1. Pour boiling water over the coconut in a large bowl. Stir, allow to stand. When cool mix with hands and squeeze the coconut to extract the juice.
2. Strain with a fine sieve or a muslin cloth, press or squeeze. This mixture will extract 1½ cups of coconut milk. It can be used when canned milk is not available.

CREME FRAICHE

Ingredients:
300ml thickened cream
300ml sour cream
Method:
1. Combine both ingredients in a bowl, cover and let it stand at room temperature until the mixture becomes thick.
Or
2 parts butter milk
1 part milk
Method:
Mix well. Allow to stand overnight. The mixture will thicken.

SPROUTS

Sprouts are easy to make. The simple elements of light and water make seeds grow.
Method:
1. Place a few tbsp of mung bean seeds in a clear glass jar or bowl. Allow to soak overnight.
2. Remove excess water, rinse and allow to stand. Cover the top of the jar with a light muslin cloth.
3. Rinse and drain every day. Sprouts will be ready in 3-5 days.

EGG – SUBSTITUTE
½ cup sour milk or yogurt for every egg (1)
Or
1 tbsp vinegar for every egg (1)

TORTILLAS

Tortillas are made with wheat flour or powdered corn (Masa mix)
Wheat flour tortillas:

Ingredients:
2 cups (300g) plain flour
1 tsp salt
50g margarine
¾ cup warm water

Method:
1. Sift flour and salt in a bowl. Rub in margarine. Stir in enough water to make a soft dough.
2. Knead dough well on a floured surface for about 10min. or until smooth and elastic. Cover dough and stand for 1hr.
3. Divide dough into 12 pieces. Roll each on lightly floured surface until about 20cm circle.
4. Cook tortillas on a heated griddle pan (thava), one at a time, until underside is flecked with brown bubbles. This shows that the dough is cooked on 1 side. Greece pan lightly and turn tortilla to cook on the other side. Remove from heat and cover with a tea towel to keep warm till required.
5. They are used as wraps with filling inside.

Potatoes

"It is easy to halve the potato where there is love."
— Irish Proverb

SOME - FACTS

Potato flesh is either white or cream to yellowish.
Yellow fleshed potatoes have a smooth creamy texture. Sometimes referred to as 'waxy'
White varieties vary from smooth to dry, floury texture.
Dry potatoes are generally better for frying (chips etc.) whereas the moisture potatoes are better for cooking and boiling.

A. OLD AND NEW:

Old or new depend on how long they are in the ground. New potatoes are harvested as soon as the plants are fully grown. Old potatoes are left in the ground for storage or to mature after the plants mature.

B.NUTRITIONAL VALUE

1. 99% fat free.
2. 367 kilojoules (90 calories) in a 200g potato or about the same as an apple.
3. It is the added oil, butter; cream and gravy that make a potato fattening and also the fats and oils they are cooked in.
4. They are an excellent source of easily digested carbohydrates plus minerals such as iron, magnesium, potassium and essential vitamins such as vitamin C and several B group vitamins.
5. Potatoes also contain a small quantity of protein.
6. Unwashed potatoes are best for storing.
7. Green skinned potatoes can be toxic.
8. Do not store potatoes in a refrigerator. Store in a cool dark place.
9. Peel just before required.
10. Peel thinly or cook in jacket. Thick peeling is wasteful and loses nutrients just under the skin. Do not soak in water for too long. Potatoes lose nutritive value if left soaking in water for too long.
11. Every country has its own variety so do check with your supplier for the names in your area.

Mineral Giving Foods

Calcium: for bone and tooth formation, heart muscle and nerve function. Found in green leafy vegetables ,tofu and broccoli.
Iron: for making myoglobin and haemoglobin. Found in dried apricots, legumes soya flour and raisins.
Iodine: for regulating the thyroid gland. Found in oats
Manganese: for osteoarthritis. Found in fortified bread.
Magnesium: for making digestive enzymes and DNA cells. Found in beans fortified cereals and green vegetables.
Phosphorus: for tooth and bone growth , nerve and muscle function. Found in dairy products and legumes.
Potassium: for healthy muscle function including the heart. Found in bananas and potatoes.
Selenium: preventing oxidation of fatty acids together with vitamin E. Found in mushrooms, garlic and onions.
Zinc: metabolism and the digestive system. Found in yogurt, wheat germ and fortified cereals.

Vitamins in a vegetarian diet

A: beta-carotine in yellow vegetables eg. carrots and butter nut
D: fortified milk, fortified margarine and sunlight
E: vegetable oils, wholegrain cereals, green leafy vegetables and nuts.
B1: whole grains, nuts and yeast.
B2: whole grains peas peanuts and milk
Niacin: whole grains legumes and nuts
Pantothenic acid: green vegetables and whole grains
B6: leafy green vegetables, whole grain cereals bananas, tomatoes and yogurt
Folic acid: leafy green vegetables
Biotin: yeast
C (ascorbic acid): citrus fruit, tomatoes, green vegetables eaten raw. Heat rapidly destroys it.

Know Some of Your Cheese

Soft and Blue cheeses.
These have a soft texture and are left to mature, from a few weeks to a few months, under controlled conditions. They have to be stored in a refrigerator.
Brie: has a mild flavor. For a cheese board and also enjoyed with bread.
Camembert: Creamy soft white. Can be crumbed and deep-fried, and used in desserts with fresh fruit.
Chavroux: Pyramid shaped cheese made from goats milk. Has a melt in the mouth flavour and can be used in stuffings for vegetables and pasta.
Boursin: French triple cream cheese flavoured with garlic and herb and black pepper. Used with bread and savoury biscuits.
Chevre: Delicate goat's cheese shaped like a log. Available plain or flavoured. Used on cheese board or with bread and savoury biscuits.
Mozzerella: Traditionally made from buffalo milk but now produced from cow's milk. Is mild and melts well. Popular for pizza topping and in salads and pasta.
Halloumi: Traditional goat's milk cheese from Cyprus. Now also made from cow's milk. Soft, rubbery and holds its shape. Can be flavoured with herbs and spices and used in salads and fried or grilled.
Fontina: Delicate, fruity flavoured Italian cheese. Used in sandwiches and salads and also melts well in pastas and stuffing.
Blue Stilton, Gorgonzola and Danish blue are blue-veined, salty, tangy and great for cheese board, soups, stuffing and sauces and also with fruit as a dessert.
Fresh Cheeses are not left to age. Fresh flavoured and soft textured. Can be used in salads, desserts, stuffing for pies, vegetables or pizza. These are mainly mascarpone, feta, cream cheese, cottage cheese and flavoured cream cheese.
Semi hard and hard cheese: Gouda, sheep gouda and boerenkaas are dutch cheeses, semi-hard and can be grated and used in sandwiches, stuffing and pasta.
Port du Salut, Gruyere, Emanthal are Swiss cheeses used in salads, sauces in sandwiches and as a dessert with fruit.
Cheddar, Bon Blanc, Wensleydale are English cheeses. Can be used for a cheese board, in salads, toppings and in baking.
Parmesan: Italian cheese matured over a year. Is a very hard cheese and can be grated and used in pasta, risotto, sauces and as a topping.
Pecorino: Is the oldest cheese. Has Roman origins and can be grated and used as toppings or added to sauces.

Uses of Nuts

Nuts deteriorate in quality so you should buy a small quantity at a time. Store in air tight containers to be used over a few weeks. Damp or mouldy nuts become toxic.

1. **Almonds:** can be eaten raw or cooked, whole, split, flaked, chopped or ground, with skin or blanched used in sweets, pastries, in baking and in salads.
2. **Walnuts:** used in baking, sweets, in savoury dishes and in salads and can be eaten raw.
3. **Pecans**: used in baking, sweet and savoury dishes, pie fillings and eaten raw in salads.
4. **Cashew nuts:** used as a snack and in Asian cooking.
5. **Macadamias:** eaten raw or used in sweets and baking.
6. **Chestnuts**: they have a short shelf life and have to be used quickly. Can be ground into flour and used in cakes and puddings.
7. **Pinenuts:** can be made into a pesto. Also used in Italian cooking, and in baking cakes and biscuits.

RECIPES

Curried Mixed Vegetables Indian Style

Preparation Time: 30 min
Cooking Time: 20min
Serves: 4 to 6

Ingredients
4 tbsp coconut or olive oil
1 onion chopped
6-8 curry leaves, chopped
1 cup sweet potatoes, cut into cubes
1 cup carrots, chopped
1 cup zucchini, cut into cubes
1 cup green beans, cut into halves
1 cup pumpkin, cut into cubes
1 cup fresh green peas
1 cup potatoes, cut into cubes
1 cup water
1 tsp turmeric
1tsp ground coriander
1tsp ground cumin
1 tsp crushed garlic
1 tsp grated ginger
3 chopped green chillies
½ cup plain yoghurt
2/3 cup fresh shredded coconut
2 tsp salt

Method
1. In a heavy based pot, sauté the onions in oil
2. Add ground cumin, chillies, turmeric powder, ground coriander, ginger, garlic, curry leaves and salt and stir.
3. Add vegetables starting with the potatoes, then carrots, sweet potatoes, green beans, peas and lastly the zucchini.
4. Add yoghurt and water. Bring to boil, lower heat to a simmer till the vegetables are soft.
5. Add shredded coconut and serve with rice

Braised Pumpkin and Potatoes

Preparation Time: 30 min
Cooking Time: 15 min
Serves: 4 to 6

Ingredients
3 Tablespoon Ghee
1 small onion, chopped
1 tsp cumin seeds
½ tsp mustard seeds
1 small cinnamon stick
2 cardamom pods
2 sticks of clove
2 curry leaves
½ tsp fenugreek seeds
2 tbsp yoghurt
450g pumpkin, cut into cubes
450g potatoes, peeled and cut into cubes
1 cup water
½ tsp turmeric
1 tsp chilli powder
1tsp ground coriander
1tsp ground cumin
1 tsp crushed garlic
1 tsp lemon juice
1 tsp sugar
2 tsp salt

Method
1. Sauté onion in ghee, add cumin, mustard, cloves, cardamom, and cinnamon
2. Add the rest of the spices and stir
3. Add potatoes and pumpkin and water. Bring to boil, lower heat and cook until soft.
4. Serve with rice or roti

Chicken flavoured Corn Soup Chinese Style

Preparation Time: 10 min
Cooking Time: 20 min
Serves: 4 to 6

Ingredients
2 litres of water
1 veg. stock cube
250g chopped soya strips
1 thumb nail size fresh ginger (thinly sliced)
4 crushed peppercorns
1 chopped onions
3 sprigs of parsley
1 tsp salt
475g can cream corn
1 tsp salt
4 tbsp corn flour
4 tbsp water
1 tsp sesame oil
5 shallots
1 tsp grated ginger
4 chopped shallots for garnishing

Method
1. Dissolve stock cube in water.
2. Soak chicken strips in some water.
3. Sauté half the onions in sesame oil till tender.
4. Make a paste of the corn flour and water.
5. Add all ingredients except the corn flour paste and the ginger and shallot set aside for garnishing.
Boil for 10 minutes.
6. Now add the corn flour paste and stir until the soup thickens.
7. Garnish with grated ginger and chopped shallot before serving.

Long - Soup

Preparation Time: 10 min
Cooking Time: 30 min
Serves: 4 to 6

Ingredients
1 tbsp cooking oil
6 cups water
2 vegetable stock cubes
250g shredded mixed vegetable.
¼ tsp grated ginger
1 ½ tsp soy sauce
125g clear rice noodles
3 chopped shallots for garnishing

Method:
1. In a deep pot dissolve stock cubes in water and bring to boil.
2. In a wok, using 1 tbsp oil stir fry the vegetables. Add ginger and soy sauce.
3. Add to pot of water and boil for 10 minutes.
4. In a separate pot cook noodles in salted boiling water for 5 to 10 minutes.
5. To serve, place noodles in soup bowl and pour hot soup on them. Sprinkle chopped shallots on top to garnish.

Chop-Suey Vegetables with Soya prawns or Soya chicken strips

Preparation Time: 1½ hour
Cooking Time: 20 min
Serves: 4 to 6

Ingredients
Marinade for Soya prawns or Soya chicken strips.
2 tablespoon Soya sauce
2 tablespoon brown vinegar
2 tablespoon sugar
1 tsp ginger paste
1 tsp crushed garlic.
Mix all the ingredients and marinate the Soya prawns or chicken strips.
Vegetables:
1 Cup finely sliced Chinese cabbage
125g sliced green beans
2 diagonally sliced celery sticks
2 sliced onions.
1 carrot cut into very small cubes
2 tablespoon of cooking oil
2 tablespoon corn flour
1 tbsp Soy sauce
240g bamboo shoots
1 vegetable stock cube
1 cup water
Salt and pepper to taste

Method:
1. Marinate chicken strips or prawns for 1 hour.
2. Heat oil in a pan and stir-fry chicken strips or prawns with the vegetables. Toss in pan till all ingredients are well combined. Cook for about 5 minutes.
3. Combine water, stock cube, corn flour and bamboo shoots and then cook for a further 5 minutes stirring constantly.
4. Remove from heat. Serve with rice.

RICE: Read and follow cooking instructions on the packet of rice.
NOODLES: can be boiled and set aside. Heat before serving.
NB. In China the preparation time is longer than the cooking time as there was a shortage of fuel. Food had to be cooked quickly and eaten fresh.

Fried Green Beans – Thai Style

Preparation Time: 10 min
Cooking Time: 10 min
Serves: 4 to 6

Ingredients:
1 tbsp peanut oil
2 tbsp crushed garlic
1 tbsp grated fresh ginger
2 chopped spring onions
2 tbsp Worcestershire sauce
1 chopped green chilli
2 tbsp rice vinegar
2 tsp sugar

Method
1. Fry green beans in hot oil for 3 to 4 min. Remove from oil when just turning brown.
2. Heat oil in a wok. Add green chilli, spring onions, garlic and ginger and cook for 1min.
3. Add the beans and the water, sauce, vinegar and sugar and stir fry for 2 to 3 min.
4. Serve immediately.

Thai Vegetable Curry

Preparation Time: 20 min.
Cooking Time: 20 min
Serves: 4 to 6

Ingredients:
4 tbsp oil
2 cloves
3 black peppercorns
1 cup chopped onions
2 tbsp crushed garlic
2 tbsp chopped lemon grass
2 tbsp lemon juice
2 tbsp chopped lime leaves
2 tbsp chopped spring onions
1 tsp crushed green chillies
1 tsp grated fresh ginger
1 tsp salt
2 cups coconut milk
400g fried tofu
2 tbsp brown sugar
500g prepared vegetables (cut and diced)
3 tbsp soy sauce

Method:
1. Make a marinade of soy sauce, sugar, lemon juice, crushed garlic, ginger, lemon grass, green chillies, salt and lime leaves. Marinate vegetables in this mixture.
2. Dry roast cloves, coriander seeds, peppercorns, cumin seeds, cinnamon in a pan on moderate heat. Remove from heat and grind in a pepper mill or in a mortar and pestle when cold.
3. Sauté the onions in oil. Add marinated vegetables, spices, and coconut milk. Bring to boil and simmer until cooked. Serve with rice.

Desserts

Banana Fritters

Preparation Time: 20 min
Cooking Time: 30 min
Serves: 4 to 6
Ingredients:
2 cups self-raising flour
½ cup water
1½ cups water
4 bananas
Oil for deep frying
Method:
1. Sieve flour and bicarbonate of soda in a bowl. Add water and mix to a smooth batter.
2. Drop banana pieces into batter. Deep fry in hot oil. Dry on absorbent paper.
3. Serve with ice cream.

Sesame-Peanut Candy

Preparation Time: 20 min
Cooking Time: 20 min
Serves: 4 to 6

Ingredients
2 cups sugar
$\frac{1}{3}$ cup white vinegar
1 tbsp water
½ cup toasted sesame seeds
1½ cups unsalted peanuts

Method:
1. Combine the sugar vinegar and water together in a saucepan. Stir over low heat until the sugar dissolves. Bring to boil. Do not stir.
2. Boil for 10min until golden brown. To test, drop a little toffee into cold water. If it turns into a hard ball, it is ready.
3. Prepare a baking tray by greasing it. Pour ½ the sesame seeds spread in the tray. Pour and spread all the peanuts on top of the sesame seeds.
4. Pour the hot toffee on top of the nuts. Smooth surface with the back of an oiled wooden spoon. Sprinkle the rest of the sesame seeds on the toffee while still hot.
5. Cut candy into strips when it is completely cool.

Cheese Crescent Pastries

Preparation time: 30 min
Cooking Time: 30 min
Serves: 4 to 6

Ingredients:
2 cups flour
1 tsp baking powder
¼ cup oil
¾ cup milk
½ tsp salt

Filling:
1 cup grated feta cheese
2 tablespoon finely chopped parsley
1 boiled mashed potato
40g cream cheese

Method:
1. Sift flour baking powder and salt.
2. Rub oil into the flour till mixture is like fine breadcrumbs.
3. Add milk and knead into soft dough.
4. Roll out on to a floured board. Cut into 8 inch rounds.
5. Mix filling ingredients all together.
6. Drop a rounded tsp of filling into the centre of rounds of pastry. Double to close forming ½ moons shapes. Seal edges.
7. Deep fry well sealed crescents till light brown in colour.
8. Drain on paper towel to remove excess oil. Serve hot.
PS This recipe can be used with other fillings also, (both sweet and savoury) and served as a teatime snack.

Felafel –Middle Eastern Way

Preparation Time: 20 min
Cooking Time: 30 min
Serves: 4 to 6

Ingredients:
1 tbsp olive oil
1 medium onion - finely chopped
1 clove garlic - crushed
2 medium potatoes –boiled and mashed.
1 tin chick peas (450g) drained
1 tsp ground cinnamon
1 tsp cumin powder
½ cup chopped parsley
Some plain flour
Vegetable oil for deep frying

Yogurt Dip
1 small green cucumber - finely chopped
1 cup plain yogurt
½ tsp cumin powder
2 tablespoon chopped fresh mint
¼ tsp salt

Method:
Falafel
1. Sauté onions in 1 tbsp olive oil till soft.
2. Process all ingredients until smooth.
3. Drop rounded tablespoon of mixture in a baking tray and place in a refrigerator till required for frying for about an hour.
4. Roll into balls and toss into flour and deep-fry till browned. Drain on paper towel. Serve with dip.

DIP:
Mix all ingredients together in a serving bowl. Serve with falafel balls.

Soya Tangine with Dates and Honey

Preparation Time: 30 min
Cooking Time: 30 min
Serves: 4 to 6

Ingredients:
500g soya chunks, soaked overnight in warm water
1 tablespoon olive oil
1 medium onions –finely chopped
4 cloves crushed garlic
1 tsp ground fresh ginger
1 tsp ground cumin seeds
1 tsp ground coriander
1 tsp turmeric powder
1 tsp cinnamon powder
1 tsp chillies powder
1 and a half cups vegetable stock
1 cup water
½ cup seedless dates
¼ cup honey
½ blanched almonds
1 tbsp coriander leaves for garnishing

Method:
1. Soya chunks have to be washed and covered with warm water to rehydrate.
2. In a tbsp of oil sauté onions till soft. Add spices and garlic and ginger stirring all the time.
3. Add soya chunks and cover with stock. Simmer till mixture thickens, about 30min. Stir in dates honey and nuts.
4. Garnish with coriander and serve with Naan bread or rice.
NB. Use a heavy based non-stick pot or tagine pot to prepare this dish. It is usually a special occasions' dish.

Egg Plant (Brinjal) with Pumpkin and Feta Cheese

Preparation Time: 1 hour
Cooking Time: 20 min
Serves: 4 to 6

Ingredients:
4 medium sized egg plants, cut into halves lengthwise. Sprinkle with coarse salt

200g pieces of pumpkin finely chopped
1 cloves garlic, crushed
1 tsp ground cumin
1 tsp ground coriander
1 tbsp brown sugar
1 cup cooked long rice
2 tbsp chopped fresh coriander leaves
1/3 cup toasted nuts (pecan, hazel or almonds)
100g feta cheese-crumbled

Method:
1. Allow salt to stand inside egg plant for 30 min. Rinse egg plant and pat dry. Brush with half the oil and place on wire rack on baking tray. Bake for 40min at 180°F till egg plant is cooked. Cool for 10min. Scoop flesh from centre of egg plant, shells for filling.
2. Heat remaining oil in a pan and add pumpkin onion garlic and spices and stir fry till pumpkin is tender. Add egg plant flesh sugar rice coriander and nuts.
3. Divide mixture and fill eggplant shells, top with cheese. Bake uncovered in moderate oven until cheese is lightly browned.

Okra with Baby Onion and Tomatoes

Preparation Time: 10 min
Cooking Time: 35 min
Serves: 4 to 6

Ingredients:
500g okra
¼ cup olive oil
2 cloves garlic, crushed
2 teaspoons cumin powder
2 teaspoons ground cinnamon
½ tsp ground allspice
450g chopped tomatoes
2 cups vegetable stock

Method:
1. Trim stems of okra. Do not puncture okra.
2. Heat half the oil in a pan. Add onions and cook, stirring occasionally until onions are browned. Remove onions and set aside.
3. Add remaining oil. Heat, add okra and spices. Stirfry till lightly browned.
4. Return onions to pan. Add stock and tomatoes and simmer for ½ an hour till okra is soft and tomato mixture is thickened.
5. Serve with rice.

Tabhouleh Bulgar Wheat Salad

Preparation Time: 15 min
Serves: 4 to 6

Ingredients:
$^2/_3$ cup bulgur wheat
4 cups flat, leafed parsley or shredded lettuce
½ cup chopped mint
4 large tomatoes chopped
2 medium onions, chopped
¾ cup olive oil
½ cup fresh lemon juice
½ tsp coarse black pepper
Salt to taste

Method:
1. Cover bulgur wheat with cold water. Stand for 15min. Drain and press water out.
2. Add remaining ingredients and mix until combined.

Cucumber with Minted Yogurt

Preparation Time: 10 min
Serves: 4 to 6

Ingredients:
1 small english cucumber
2 cups plain yogurt
¼ cup fresh chopped mint
1 clove garlic, crushed
½ tsp cumin powder
1 tbsp lemon juice

Method:
1. Halve cucumber, scoop out the seeds and chop fine.
2. Combine all ingredients and serve after refrigerating for one hour.

Pear and Cashew Nut Pudding (similar to Baklava)

Preparation Time: 20 min
Cooking Time: 30 min
Serves: 8

Ingredients:
2 sheets ready rolled puff pastry
1½ cups chopped dried pears
½ cup sultanas
1 cup unsalted roasted cashew nuts - finely chopped
1 tsp grated lemon rind
400g sweetened condensed milk
2¼ cup milk
¼ cup brown sugar
½ tsp ground cinnamon
½ tsp ground cardamom
½ cup yogurt
1 tbsp corn flour

Method:
1. Bake sheets of pastry in 3 separate trays till risen and brown.
2. Grease an oven proof dish, 4 litres capacity.
3. Crumble 1 sheet of pastry at the bottom of dish evenly. Sprinkle with half the pears, half the sultanas and 1/3 of the nuts. Repeat layering process.
4. Top with remaining pastry and nuts.
5. Bake in a moderately slow oven, 150°C for 30min or until top is browned and pudding is set.
6. Serve with fresh cream or ice-cream.

Kheer – Rice pudding with cashews and pistachios

Preparation Time: 10 min
Cooking Time: 45 min
Serves: 4 to 6

Ingredients:
1 cups milk
¼ cup honey
¾ cup white short grained rice
¼ cup dried sultanas or currants
1 tbsp chopped unsalted cashews, toasted
1 tbsp toasted pistachios, chopped
1 whole cardamom pods

Method:
1. Combine milk and honey in a large pan. Stir over heat until honey is melted. Bring to boil.
2. Add rice currants and cardamom to pan. Simmer uncovered, for about 45min or until rice is tender and mixture is thick, stirring occasionally. Serve with cream and extra honey if desired.

Mexican – Tacos (similar to roti rolls)

Preparation Time: 20 min
Cooking Time: 10 min
Serves: 4 to 6

Ingredients:
6-20cm tortillas or rotis
1 tbsp vegetable oil
2 green shallots, chopped
2 medium roasted or raw tomatoes-chopped
¾ cup cooked beans
¼ cup shredded lettuce
¼ cup sour cream

Guacamole:
2 medium avocados, peeled and mashed
1 small chopped tomato
2 tsps lemon juice
1 small mild chopped chillies
1 green shallot, chopped
1 tsp chopped coriander
Mix all guacamole ingredients together. Add salt to taste.

Method:
1. Sauté shallots in oil until shallots are soft. Add beans and stir for five minutes.
2. Add tomatoes and stir fry for a further five minutes. Add salt and pepper to taste.
3. Using a heavy based pan or griddle (thava) warm the tortillas on both sides.
4. Serve tortillas with bean mixture in the centre, top with guacamole, sour cream and lettuce. Wrap on both sides like a roll to enclose filling.
5. Serve as a starter.

Nachos (Pizza Type Tortillas)

Preparation Time: 20 min
Cooking Time: 30 min
Serves: 4 to 6

Ingredients:
4 - 20cm tortillas
Vegetable oil for deep frying
½ cup hot tomato sauce or salsa
1 large tomatoes, peeled, seeded and chopped
½ tsp ground cumin
1 small chopped green chilli
1 cup cooked beans
2 green shallots, chopped
½ cup grated cheddar cheese
½ cup red Leicester cheese

Method:
1. Cut each tortilla into 8 triangles. Deep fry in hot oil until browned. Drain.
2. Combine salsa, coriander, cumin and chillies in a bowl. Mix well.
3. Start spreading a tsp of beans triangle with 2 tsps of tomato mixture and sprinkle evenly with shallot and cheeses. 4. Place triangles on baking tray and grill till cheese melts.
5. Serve as starters.

Roasted Peppers with Cheese

Preparation Time: 20 min
Cooking Time: 30 min
Serves: 4 to 6

Ingredients:
1 tbsp olive oil
1 medium onion sliced
3 medium peppers roasted peeled and sliced
200g mixed vegetables for stir frying
1 small green chilli, chopped
2 cloves garlic, crushed
400g mozzarella cheese, sliced
3 tablespoons fresh chopped coriander

Method:
1. Heat oil in a pan. Add onions and vegetables. Cook stirring until soft.
2. Add red peppers garlic chopped chilli salt and pepper to taste and stir fry until vegetables are cooked dry.
3. Place vegetables in an oven proof dish
4. Top vegetables with cheese and bake uncovered till cheese begins to bubble.
5. Sprinkle with coriander and serve with tortillas.

Marinated Vegetables (Salad)

Preparation Time: 20 min
Cooking Time: 45 min
Serves: 4 to 6

Ingredients:
1 medium red pepper
1 fresh corn cob
200g green beans, halved
200g patty pans (yellow squash)
1½ cups frozen peas
8 baby potatoes halved
1 bunch red radishes, stalks and tails removed
¼ cup fresh chopped coriander leaves

Dressing:
½ cup olive oil
1 medium onion, finely chopped
2 cloves crushed garlic
2 small fresh red chillies, seeded and finely chopped
½ tsp ground cumin
¼ cup white wine vinegar
1 tsp grated lemon rind
2 tablespoons chopped fresh oregano

Method:
1. Boil or steam potatoes, squash, beans, peas and corn kernels. Corn can be cut off the cob. Each vegetable must be boiled separately.
2. Rinse under cold water and drain.
3. Add radishes to pan of boiling water and return to boil. Drain immediately and rinse under cold water and drain.
4. Combine vegetables together in a bowl.
5. Combine all dressing ingredients and mix well.
6. Pour dressing over vegetables and refrigerate for 1 hour.
7. Another way to prepare the dressing:
8. Heat oil in a pan. Add onion, garlic, chillies and cumin. Cook stirring until onion is soft. Cool.
9. Combine vinegar, rind, juice and oregano. Add onion mixture on the vegetables and mix well.

Poached Guavas in Spicy Syrup

Preparation Time: 20 min
Cooking Time: 1 hour
Serves: 4 to 6

Ingredients:
1 lime grated rind and 1 tbsp of juice
1 ½ cups sugar (330g)
1 cinnamon stick
5 cloves
2 ½ cups (625ml)
4 medium guavas
½ tsp vanilla essence

Method:
1. Using a vegetable peeler, peel rind of lemon thinly and cut into strips.
2. Peel guavas and cut in halves and scoop out seeds.
3. Make sugar syrup by combining and stirring over heat without boiling the lemon juice, sugar water and cinnamon in a pan, until sugar is dissolved. Cover and simmer for about 20 minutes.
4. Add guavas to sugar syrup and simmer for a further 10minutes.
5. Remove guavas and throw away the cinnamon stick.
6. Simmer syrup until reduced to about 1¼ cups for about 10 minutes.
7. Stir in essence and pour over guavas. Cover and refrigerate.
8. Serve with ice cream.

SOUTH AFRICAN-STYLE

Butter Nut Soup

Preparation time: 15 min
Cooking Time: 30 min
Serves: 6

Ingredients:
500g butter nut, cleaned and cubed
1 large onion (chopped)
2 tbsp butter
1 tbsp oil
½ cup fresh cream
1 tsp chopped fresh thyme
½ tsp cumin seeds
1 small stick cinnamon
2 cups milk
1 tsp chopped parsley to garnish
1 tsp salt
½ tsp crushed black pepper

Method:
1. Braise or sauté the onions in the butter and oil. Add cumin seeds and cinnamon.
2. When the onions turn light brown, add the butter nut and cook for 5 min.
3. Add milk and bring to boil. Lower heat and the butter nut to cook till tender.
4. Remove from heat, cool and liquidise the soup in a blender. Pour soup back into pan. Add thyme, salt and pepper and simmer for about 5 min.
5. Pour into soup bowl. Add a dollop of cream in the centre and garnish with a sprig of parsley.
6. Serve hot with crusty bread.

Mixed Vegetable Soup

Preparation Time: 30 min
Cooking Time: 30 min
Serves: 6

Ingredients:
500g mixed vegetable finely chopped
¼ cup oil
1 onion finely chopped
2 cloves garlic crushed
1 tsp fresh ground ginger
1 tbsp chopped fresh herbs (thyme parsley rosemary)
2 tbsp Worcestershire sauce
1 tbsp jam, any flavour
2 tbsp tomato paste
1 tsp salt
1 tsp crushed black pepper

Method:
1. Sauté onions in oil.
2. Add all ingredients in a large pan and stir fry for 5 min
3. Add 6 cups of water and bring to boil.
4. When it boils, lower heat and cook until vegetables are cooked very soft.
5. Serve with crusty bread or bread rolls.

Babotie Soya Mince and Mixed Vegetables

Preparation Time: 45 min
Cooking Time: 30 min
Serves: 6

Ingredients:
1 cup soya mince
1½ cups water
1 tsp salt
1 tsp cumin seeds
1 piece cinnamon (thumb nail size)
25 ml butter
1 tsp turmeric powder
1 tsp coriander powder
1 tsp ground fresh ginger
1 tsp fresh crushed garlic
1 stick cinnamon
2 cloves
3 bay leaves
3 lemon leaves
3 cardamom pods
2 tbsp tomato paste
1 thick slice of bread
250ml milk
50ml lemon juice
75g seedless raisins
10 almonds
1 grated fresh apple
10 dried apricots
1 green chilli chopped
2 tablespoons sugar

Method:
1. Soak soya mince in 1½ cups of water for 10 min.
2. Sauté the onions in butter till soft.
3. Add the salt, cinnamon cloves, cardamom and fry for 5 min. add the chilli powder, green chillies, turmeric powder, coriander powder, cumin powder, ginger and garlic and tomato paste and cook for 2min.
4. Add drained mince and cook for a further 5 min till well blended.
5. Add fruit (apples raisins, almonds) and sugar.
6. Soak the bread in the milk.
7. Pour mixture from pot into a casserole dish. Cover evenly with 1 cup of water.
8. Push bay leaves and lemon leaves evenly into mixture.
9. Using a fork mix the soaked bread and spread over the mince. Sprinkle black pepper over it.
10. Bake in a moderate oven (180°C) for about 30min.
11. Serve with rice or bread.

Vegetable Stew with Dumplings

Preparation Time: 30min
Cooking Time: 1 hour
Serves: 6-8

Ingredients:
500g vegetable chunks (cubed potatoes, butternut, or pumpkin, cabbage green beans and peas)
2 onions
¼ cup oil
2 tbsp butter
2 tbsp Worcestershire sauce
1 tbsp apricot jam
1 tsp salt
½ tsp black pepper
1 tsp fresh ground ginger
1 tsp crushed garlic
1 tbsp chopped fresh parsley
1 tbsp fresh chopped thyme

Method:
1. Sauté the onions in the oil and butter.
2. Add the tomato, Worcestershire sauce, salt, black pepper, ginger and garlic and half the water together with the vegetables into the pot. Bring to boil and cook for 20min.
3. Add thyme and apricot jam and simmer for 5min.

Dumplings

Ingredients:
1½ cups self-raising flour
½ tsp salt
2 tablespoons oil or butter
1 tsp mixed herbs -thyme and parsley
½ tsp ground black pepper

Method:
1. Add salt, pepper oil and herbs to the flour. Use the water to make a soft dough.
2. Using wet hands make equal sized balls.
3. Add the rest of the water to the stew and bring to boil. Drop the dumpling balls on top of the boiling stew and cover the pot.
4. Lower the heat and cook until the dumplings are double the size. Do not stir.
5. Serve stew with dumplings in deep bowls. Garnish with parsley.

Roast Vegetables

Preparation Time: 30min
Cooking Time: 30min
Serves 6

Ingredients:
250g broccoli
250 g green beans, topped and tailed
250 g carrots, cut in chunks
250 g cubed butternut or pumpkin
250 g potatoes peeled and quartered
1 tbsp mixed herbs, (thyme, parsley and rosemary)
2 tbsp worcestershire sauce
½ cup water
1 tsp black pepper
1 tsp crushed garlic
1 chopped onion

Method:
1. Mix salt, pepper crushed garlic, melted butter, mixed herbs, and onion to make a marinade.
2. Rub to coat marinade on all the vegetables.
3. Spread vegetables on an oven tray. Pour left over marinade and water into the tray. Cover with foil.
4. Roast at 180°C for 30 min.

Frickedels using Fry's Soya Mince

Preparation Time: 30 min
Cooking Time: 45 min
Serves: 4 to 6

Ingredients:
2 cups Fry's soya mince
2 tbsp cake flour
1 tbsp Worcestershire sauce
1Tbsp chopped fresh parsley
1 tbsp chopped fresh thyme
2 tbsp tomato paste
1 tsp crushed black pepper
1 onion finely chopped
½ cup bread crumbs
2 tablespoons butter
1 tsp fresh garlic crushed
1 tsp salt
½ tsp cumin powder

Method:
1. Combine all ingredients and knead together till mixture resembles dough.
2. Break little bits and form balls.
3. In a heavy based pan sauté 1 chopped onion in 2 tbsp of oil.
4. Fry the meatballs gently till they are brown in colour.
5. Serve as meat balls with roast vegetables or
6. Place in a casserole dish, add 2 cups of stock and bake in an oven for 30 min at 180°C
7. Serve with rice or bread.

Fry's Sausages (Soya)

Preparation Time: 15 min
Cooking Time: 15 min
Serves: 6

Ingredients
¼ cup water
½ cup oil
1 packet of Fry's sausages
½ tsp coriander powder
½ tsp cumin powder
1 tsp crushed garlic
2 tbsp butter
2 tbsp Worcestershire sauce
1 chopped onion
½ tsp crushed black pepper
1 tsp chopped fresh rosemary

Method:
1. Make marinade by mixing coriander powder, cumin powder, crushed garlic, Worcestershire sauce, butter, black pepper and rosemary. Allow to stand for 15 min.
2. In a pan sauté the onions till they turn a pale brown.
3. Fry the sausages in the same pan for 3min. Add the water and heat for 1 min. When water boils lower heat, cover and cook for a further 5min.
4. Serve with mashed potatoes.

Pumpkin Fritters

Preparation time: 30min
Cooking Time: 30min
Serves: 6

Ingredients:
2 cups boiled pumpkin –mashed
1 cup cake flour
2 tsp baking powder
¼ cup cinnamon sugar-(powdered cinnamon mixed with sugar)
½ tsp cinnamon powder
½ cups Sugar
¼ cup melted butter
Oil for deep frying

Method:
1. Combine flour, baking powder, melted butter, cinnamon powder, and sugar together. Make into a soft batter.
2. Heat oil in a pan to fry fritters.
3. Drop teaspoons full into pan and fry until golden brown and well risen.
4. Remove from oil and dredge with cinnamon sugar while still hot.
5. Serve with tea.

Milk Tart

Preparation Time: 45 min
Cooking Time: 1hr
Serves: 6

Ingredients
Pastry:
2 cups flour
½ cup melted butter
2 tsp baking powder
½ cup sugar
2tbsps chick pea flour
¼ cup milk

Method for pastry:
1. Sift flour, baking powder and chick pea flour together.
2. Mix melted butter and sugar together.
3. In a bowl mix all ingredients. Add milk and make into dough.
4. Use a tart plate or tray and spread the dough evenly at the bottom and on the sides of the tray.
5. Bake in a preheated oven 180°C till a golden brown in colour about 25 min. Remove from oven, press down the middle while still hot if has risen too much. Allow to cool.

Filling:
Ingredients:
1½ cups milk
1 teaspoon vanilla essence
3 tablespoon flour
1 tbsp almond powder (Optional)

Method:
1. Mix ½ cup milk with vanilla and flour.
2. In a pan warm the rest of the milk and bring to boil.
3. Add hot milk into bowl with flour mixture stirring all the time.
4. When mixture is smoothly blended, return to pan and bring to boil stirring all the time.
5. Stir milk mixture until it thickens. Pour into tart shell and allow to cool.
6. Garnish with a sprinkling of cinnamon powder or grated chocolate.

SOUTH AFRICAN-- TRADITIONAL ZULU STYLE

Vegetable Chakalaka

Preparation Time: 30 min
Cooking Time: 40 min
Serves: 6

Ingredients:
500g frozen mixed vegetables
½ cup water
1can chopped tomatoes
1 can baked beans
2 chopped onions
1 chopped green chilli
1 cup green yellow and yellow pepper, chopped into chunks
2 tablespoons green coriander chopped, for garnish
1 tsp cumin seeds
1 tsp chilli powder
1 tsp coriander powder
1 tsp salt
1 tsp turmeric powder
1 tsp crushed garlic
1 tsp ground fresh ginger
¼ cup cooking oil
1 thumb nail size cinnamon sticks

Method:
1. Sauté onions in oil adding the cinnamon and cumin seeds.
2. Adding a little water make a paste of the turmeric powder, chillies powder, coriander powder, ginger, garlic and salt. Add to oil and stir for 1 min.
3. Add vegetables and water. Bring to boil. Lower the heat and cook till vegetables are soft.
4. Add canned tomatoes, baked beans and peppers. Cook for 10min on low heat.
5. The curry has a bright and colourful appearance----hence the name----Chakalaka.
6. Serve with rice or Putu.

Putu or Krummel – Pap – Made of Maize Meal South Africa

Preparation Time: 10 min
Cooking Time: 30 min
Serves: 6

Ingredients:
3 tbsp of butter
3 Cups Mealie Meal (maize meal)
3 Cups water
2 tsp salt

Method:
1. Using a heavy based pan bring water to boil. Add salt and butter, and lastly the mealie meal.
2. Use a wooden spoon and stir the meal into the water.
3. Immediately lower the heat and allow to cook for 10 minutes.
4. Stir the meal to break up the lumps until they resemble bread crumbs.
5. Allow to cook for another 10min.
6. Serve in place of rice.

Stiff Pap (Maize Porridge)

Preparation Time: 10 min
Cooking Time: 20 min
Serves: 6

Ingredients:
1 cup mealie meal (maize meal)
1 Tsp salt
1 tbsp butter
3 cups water

Method:
1. In a large pot bring 2 cups of the water to boil. Add butter and salt.
2. In a bowl mix the meal with 1 cup of water to farm a paste.
3. Add the paste to the boiling water in the pot stirring all the time until the porridge is smooth and thick. Lower the heat and allow to cook for 5min.
4. In a greased tray pour out the porridge smoothing out the surface.
5. Cut into squares and serve instead of mash or rice.

Isijabaan pap with Cabbage

Preparation Time: 15 min
Cooking Time: 30 min
Serves: 6

Ingredients:
1 small cabbage-shredded
2 tbsp butter or margarine
1 tsp salt
¼ tsp ground black pepper
2 cups mealie meal (maize meal)
2 cups water

Method:
1. Melt butter in a heavy based pan. Stir fry cabbage for about 5min.
2. Add salt and pepper and water and bring to boil.
3. Add mealie meal and stir quickly with a wooden spoon. Lower the temperature and allow to cook for 10 min.
4. Stir the cooked food to break up the one solid piece into little lumps.
5. Serve as bread or rice.

Moroccan – (Wild Spinach)

Preparation Time: 15 min
Cooking Time: 20 min
Serves: 4- 6

Ingredients:
2 packets Moroccan herbs or 2 bunches of spinach (Swiss chard)
1 large onion chopped
1 green chilli
2 cloves of garlic crushed
3 tablespoons cooking oil
Salt and pepper to taste

Method:
1. Sauté the onions in the oil till onions soften.
2. Add salt and pepper, green chilli and garlic and cook for 1min.
3. Add the herbs and stir-fry for another min.
4. Add water, turn the temperature down and cover. Cook until all the liquid is gone. Do not dry out.
Remove from cooker and leave it covered until required.

Fruit Salad

Preparation Time: 30 min
Serves: 6- 8

Ingredients:
1 pawpaw
2 apples
1 bunch of grapes
2 oranges
2 bananas
½ cup sugar
250 ml fruit juice
Fresh mint leaves for garnishing

Method:
1. Peel and deseed pawpaw. Chop into very small cubes.
2. Peel core and grate apples.
3. Peel and deseed grapes.
4. Peel and chop oranges into tiny pieces.
5. Peel and slice bananas.
6. Cut granadillas and scoop out insides.
7. Combine all prepared fruit together in a bowl. Add sugar and juice.
8. Serve with ice cream or condensed cream. Garnish with fresh mint leaves.

Nguntyatta

Preparation Time: 30 min
Cooking Time: 30 min
Serves: 6-8

Ingredients:
2 cups flour
2g instant yeast
½ tsp salt
5 tbsp sugar
1½ cups warm water
2 tbsp oil or melted butter
½ tsp vanilla essence
Oil for deep frying

Method:
1. Sift cake flour, yeast and salt together.
2. In a small bowl mix warm water sugar, oil and essence together.
3. Allow to stand, covered, in a warm place.
4. When the dough has risen to double the size, knock the dough down and knead again. Mould into marble size balls and allow to rise on a floured surface.
5. When well risen, fry in deep oil till golden brown.
6. Dredge with castor sugar while still warm.
7. Serve with tea.

Mixed Vegetable Pickle

Preparation Time: 30 min
Cooking Time: 30 min
Serves: 6-8

Ingredients:
500g shredded green beans
500 g finely sliced carrots
500 g shredded cabbage
or mixed vegetables of your choice
1 tbsp chilli powder
1tbsp mustard powder
2 tbsp crushed fresh garlic
1 tsp coriander powder
1 tsp cumin powder
1 tbsp salt
1tsp turmeric powder
1 tsp mustard seeds
1 cup brown vinegar
½ cup cooking oil
2 tbsp brown sugar
250 g mixed dried fruit (apricots, pears apples etc)

Method:
1. Put all the vegetables in a bowl and sprinkle 2 tablespoons of salt on them. Allow to stand for 24 hrs.
2. Mixing occasionally. This process dehydrates vegetables so pickle keeps longer.
3. Rinse and drain vegetables. Dry with a kitchen towel.
4. Mix all the spices; add ½ cup vinegar, oil, brown sugar. Beat with a spoon and set aside.
5. Cut finely the dried fruit and soak with ½ cup of vinegar.
6. In a large bowl toss vegetables into the spice mixture. Add prepared dried fruit and mix well. Let it stand, covered overnight.
7. Bottle and use as desired.

Lemon or Lime Pickle (My father-in-law Murray Juan's Recipe)

Preparation Time: 1hr
Cooking Time: 1hr

Ingredients:
3 large onions, chopped
1 bunch of shallots, chopped
2 tablespoons of curry leaves, chopped
1 green chilli, cut into large pieces
2 cinnamon sticks
4 cloves
4 cinnamon pods
1 tbsp whole cumin seeds
1 tbsp coriander powder
1 tbsp crushed ginger
1 tbsp chilli powder
1 tbsp turmeric powder
1 tbsp crushed fresh garlic
1 cup cooking oil
2 cups brown vinegar
1 tsp mustard seeds
2 tsp salt
2 bay leaves

Method:
1. Using the fine side of a grater remove the zest off from the lemon or lime.
2. Throw the lemons into a pot of boiling water and boil for about 10 min. Remove and allow to cool.
3. Cut lemons into bite size pieces and remove the seeds. Seeds make the pickle bitter.
4. In a large heavy based pot, sauté the onions in oil adding the cinnamon, cloves cardamom, cumin seeds, and mustard seeds.
5. When the onions turn a pale brown add the pepper pods, chilli powder, turmeric, ground cumin, ground coriander, crushed ginger, and crushed garlic and green chillies. Cook for about 5min.until the spices are cooked.
6. Add the prepared lemons, salt, curry leaves, shallots, bay leaves, and vinegar. Bring to boil.
Lower the heat and allow to cook till lemon skins are tender, stirring occasionally.
If you bottle while hot there is no need to refrigerate. The pickle is ready to eat when it is cooked.

Fazila's Green Chilli Pickle

Ingredients:
500g. green chillies, chopped
½ cup cooking oil
1 tbsp cumin seeds
1 tbsp sesame seeds
1 tbsp crushed garlic
½ cup methi pickle masala
½ cup brown vinegar
½ cup tomato sauce (ketchup)
1 table spoon salt
250 g red tamarind
2 cups water

Method:
1. Fry green chillies, cumin seeds, and sesame seeds in hot oil for 2 min.
2. Add crushed oil, methi pickle masala, vinegar, tomato sauce and salt. Mix.
3. Remove from heat.
4. Make a marinade of: tamarind and water. Mix and strain juice.
5. Pour over chillies and bottle.

Diabetic Mayonnaise

Ingredients:
125g low fat cottage cheese
175 ml low fat natural yogurt
12.5ml white wine vinegar
3ml prepared french mustard
Juice of ½ a lemon
2ml garlic salt
2ml celery salt
½ tsp freshly ground black pepper
6 drops liquid artificial sweetener

Method:
1. Place all ingredients into a food processor and blend until smooth.
2. Pour into a jar and refrigerate.
3. Stir or whisk before using.

Rocket Onion and Blue Cheese Salad – Italian Style

Preparation Time: 30 min
Cooking Time: 10 min
 Serves: 6

Ingredients:
30ml butter
30ml sugar
12 slices French bread
100g blue cheese
Balsamic vinaigrette
Bunch of small radishes (washed and trimmed)
20 pickling onions
2 sprigs of rosemary
100g rocket leaves
½ cup olive oil

Method:
1. If onions are large cut into quarters, retaining roots. Parboil for 5min.
2. Melt butter in a saucepan. Add sugar and stir. Toss onions in and continue stirring until onions are completely coated and caramelised.
3. Brush bread with olive oil and grill both sides. Place slices of blue cheese on each slice. Sprinkle with chopped rosemary.
4. Toss rocket in vinaigrette to coat.
5. Arrange in a bowl, topped with onions and radishes and surrounded with cheese and toast.

Balsamic Vinaigrette

Ingredients:
60ml balsamic vinegar
5ml dry mustard powder
Salt and pepper to taste

Method:
Whisk vinegar and seasoning together. Add oil drop by drop whisking all the time until emulsified. Add all the oil. Makes 250ml. It will keep in the refrigerator indefinitely. Use when needed.

Polenta Bread

Preparation Time: 20 min
Cooking Time: 30 min
Serves: 6

Ingredients:
250ml polenta (maize meal)
250 ml butter milk
1 tbsp chick pea flour
60 ml honey
60ml melted butter
250ml flour
10 ml baking powder
1 tsp salt
2 tbsp chopped fresh thyme and parsley

Method:
1. Preheat oven 200°C.
2. Beat chick pea flour, butter milk, honey and butter together.
3. Mix dry ingredients and herbs together in a large bowl. Make a well in the centre and pour the buttermilk mixture into it. Combine well to make dough.
4. Spread into a 20cm. Square baking tin. Bake in the centre of the oven for 30min or until golden.
5. Turn out onto rack to cool.
6. Serve with butter, cheese and olives.

Cheese Fondue

Preparation Time: 10 min
Cooking Time: 10 min
Serves: 6

Ingredients:
250g Emmentale cheese, diced
250g Gruyere cheese diced
45ml flour
1 clove garlic, crushed
500ml wine vinegar
15ml lemon juice
45 ml brandy
½ tsp ground nutmeg
½ tsp paprika
2 loaves French bread cubed. (or any crisp bread)

Method
1. Dredge the cheese with flour.
2. Pour the wine into a pot and heat at moderate temperature.
3. When the bubbles begin to rise, add the lemon juice.
4. Add the cheese, a little at a time stirring constantly with a wooden spoon until all of it is melted.
5. Add the spices and brandy. Stir to blend.
6. Transfer to fondue pot and place over a flame to keep bubbling.
7. Serve with French bread cubes. Spear the bread through the soft side into the crust-dunk and swirl in the cheese.

Grilled Broccoli and Pasta

Preparation Time: 10 min
Cooking time: 30 min
Serves: 6

Ingredients:
1 cup pasta
2 cups cauliflower or broccoli
2tbsps olive oil
1 tbsp crushed garlic
1 cup cheddar or Gouda cheese, grated
1tsp salt
1 tsp crushed black pepper
1 tbsp chopped parsley

Method:
1. Boil cauliflower or broccoli and pasta together until pasta is cooked.
2. Drain and put into a baking tray.
3. Coat with olive oil, garlic herbs salt and pepper.
4. Sprinkle with cheese and place in oven and grill until cheese melts and turns a little brown.
5. Serve while hot.

Baked Sliced Potatoes

Preparation time: 15 min
Cooking time: 40 min
Serves: 4 to 6

Ingredients:
500g potatoes thinly sliced.
175g double cream
2 tsp crushed garlic
1fennel bulb, cleaned and thinly sliced
1 chopped red chilli, deseeded
¼ cup chopped green peppers
1 tbsp chopped parsley
1 tbsp grated parmesan cheese
1 tsp salt
½ tsp crushed black pepper

Method:
1. Preheat oven to 180° C.
2. Sauté the fennel in 1 tbsp of butter.
3. Place thinly sliced potatoes in a baking tray.
4. Arrange sautéed fennel on top of potatoes. Sprinkle salt, pepper and garlic.
5. Pour cream over the potatoes. Sprinkle chopped pepper and peppers.
6. Top with parmesan and parsley.
7. Bake for 30 min. in prepared oven till potatoes are tender.
8. Serve with pasta or rice.

Vegetable Bake – Italy

Preparation Time: 30 min
Cooking time: 40 min
Serves: 6

Ingredients:
8 cups assorted vegetables cut into florets chunks or florets
½ cup butter
1 onion, chopped
¼ tsp nutmeg
½ cup flour
5cups milk
2 tsp salt
2 tsp crushed garlic
2 tbsp tomato paste
1 tsp freshly ground black pepper
250g Grated cheddar cheese
2 tbsp chopped thyme and parsley

Method:
1. Lightly steam all the vegetables separately. Some need longer than others.
2. Melt butter in a medium size saucepan. Sauté the onions in the butter. Add nutmeg, pepper and salt.
3. Stir in the flour and make a smooth paste. Gradually add more milk stirring constantly to create a sauce.
4. Remove from heat and add ½ the cheese into the sauce. Stir.
5. Continue stirring adding vegetables until all are coated.
6. Spoon into a buttered baking pan and cover with remaining cheese.
7. Bake in a preheated oven 180°C for 25min.
8. Garnish with herbs.
9. Serve with bread.

Frys Soya Sausages with tomato sauce

Preparation Time: 10 min
Cooking Time: 10 min
Serves: 4-6

Ingredients:
1 pack Fry's Soya sausages
1 can chopped tomatoes
1 large onion, chopped
1 tsp crushed garlic
1 tsp grated fresh ginger
½ tsp salt
½ tsp freshly ground black pepper
1 tsp cumin seeds
1 bay leaf
1 tsp chopped green chillies
2 tablespoons olive oil
2 tablespoons chopped fresh basil

Method:
1. Sauté onions in olive oil. Add cumin seeds and bay leaf.
2. Add ginger, garlic and green chillies. Stir.
3. Add tomatoes and sausages. Cook for 8 min.
4. Serve with rice, pasta or crusty bread.

Tuscan Tomato and Basil Sauce

Preparation Time: 10 min
Cooking Time: 20 min
Serves: 6

Ingredients:
30ml olive oil
2 cloves crushed garlic
1 onion, chopped
1 (410ml) tin chopped tomatoes
125ml red wine (optional)
2 tbsp freshly shredded basil leaves
1 tsp dried oregano
1 tbsp sugar
2 tbsp tomato paste

Method:
1. Sauté onions in olive oil until onions soften.
2. Add all ingredients except the basil and bring to boil. Lower the heat and cook for 10 min.
3. Add basil, stir and remove from heat.
4. Season with and pepper.
5. Serve chunky or puree in a processor.
6. Sauce can be used in pasta dishes or eaten with crusty bread.

Spinach and Herb Pasta Rice

Preparation time: 10 min
Cooking Time: 20 min
Serves: 4-6

Ingredients:
200 g pasta rice (Rossini)
250g baby spinach, chopped
50ml fresh dill, finely chopped
2 spring onions, finely chopped
50 ml fresh parsley, finely chopped
50ml fresh basil -finely chopped
50ml olive oil

Method:
1. Cook pasta rice according to instructions on the packet. Drain and cool by running cool water through it.
2. Combine all the ingredients in a bowl. Toss with the Rossini. Season with salt and pepper and serve.

Black Lentil Patties

Preparation Time: 10 min
Cooking Time: 20 min
Serves: 4 to 6

Ingredients:
2 cups black lentils (urad dhal), boiled
2 tbsp crushed ginger
2 tbsp grated onion
1 tsp salt
½ tsp crushed black pepper
1 tsp crushed green chillies
1 cup bread crumbs
1 tbsp chopped coriander leaves
½ cup cooking oil

Method:
1. Mix all ingredients together.
2. Make round balls and flatten in hands to form patties. Use wet hands to make work easier.
3. Fry in shallow oil.
4. Serve with a sauce.

Sweet Chilli Sauce

Preparation Time: 10 min
Cooking Time: 50 min
Makes: 750g

Ingredients:
75g red chillies, deseeded and chopped fine
6 cloves garlic, crushed
3cm piece of ginger grated
2 apples, peeled and cored
1 can (50g) chopped tomatoes
125ml apple cider vinegar
500ml (400g) sugar
125ml water
Salt to taste

Method:
1. Combine all ingredients in a sauce pan and stir until the sugar is dissolved.
2. Bring to boil and simmer for 10min stirring occasionally.
3. Puree mixture and season to taste.
4. Return mixture to pot and boil for 10 min. Pour into sterilised bottles and seal while hot.

Red Cabbage Salad

Preparation Time: 10min

Ingredients:
2 cups grated red cabbage
1 red onion, finely chopped
1 stick celery, thinly sliced

Dressing:
5 cloves garlic, crushed
1 tsp salt
½ tsp freshly ground black pepper
1 tbsp crushed roasted coriander seeds
1 tbsp honey
1 tbsp lemon juice
1 tsp Dijon mustard
2 tbsp olive oil

Method:
1. Mix the cabbage, red onion and celery into a salad bowl.
2. Crush garlic and salt together.
3. Mix olive oil, lemon juice, honey and mustard and beat together.
4. Add garlic and salt.
5. Lastly add yogurt and allow to stand.
6. When serving pour over the cabbage and toss. Dressing must not be poured early as salt makes the cabbage soft.

Potato and Beetroot Fritters

Preparation Time: 10 min
Cooking Time: 20 min
Serves: 6

Ingredients:
2 cups grated potatoes
1 cup grated beetroot
2 tbsp chopped shallots
1tsp chopped green chillies
1 tsp crushed garlic
1 tsp salt
Oil for frying

Method:
1. Mix all ingredients together to make patties.
2. Using wet hands make a round ball and flatten in palm of hand.
3. Fry in shallow oil browning both sides.
4. Serve with a sauce.

Smoked Tomato Sauce

Preparation Time: 10 min
Cooking Time: 10 min
Serves: 6

Ingredients:
500g tomatoes
1 tsp salt
½ tsp crushed black pepper
2 tbsp olive oil
2 tbsp red wine vinegar
1 tbsp sugar
Basil leaves
Black olives

Method:
1. Drizzle oil and spices on tomatoes and grill in very hot oven until they begin to change colour.
2. Remove from oven and squash tomatoes in a serving dish using a knife. Add red wine vinegar and sugar and mix roughly.
3. Tear basil leaves into the tomatoes. Mix.
4. Add black olives and serve with patties or pasta or crusty bread as a starter.

Cooked Pears served with a cream sauce

Preparation time: 10 min
Cooking Time: 10 min
Serves: 6

Ingredients:
6 firm pears
40g butter
1 tsp cinnamon powder

Method:
1. Using a potato peeler, peel pears, remove cores and cut into halves.
2. Melt butter. Place in the pan, sprinkle cinnamon and sauté until firm and tender. Remove from heat and set aside.

Sauce:
60 g butter
50ml sugar
250ml

Method:
Melt butter, add sugar, and cook over low heat until sugar becomes a light caramel colour. Stir the cream and reheat. Pour over the pears and serve warm.

Gujrathi Style – Indian

BRAISED CAULIFLOWER

Vegetable Haleem (Curried Broth) – Gujrathi Style -- Indian

Preparation Time: 10 min
Cooking Time: 1 hour
Serves: 4 to 6

Ingredients:
1cup haleem mix or (4 in 1) soup mix, pre soaked overnight
2 onion, finely chopped
2 cups frozen mixed vegetables or fresh vegetables of your choice, cleaned and dice
3 finely chopped tomatoes
1 tsp cumin seeds
1 cinnamon stick
½ tsp mustard seeds
2 cloves
2 cardamom pods
1 dry red chilli
2 bay leaves
1 sprig curry leaves
2 tablespoons chopped shallots
¼ cup cooking oil
1 tbsp mint leaves finely chopped
½ cup finely chopped coriander leaves
1 tsp coriander powder
1 tsp cumin powder
1 tsp turmeric powder
1 tsp chilli powder
½ tsp whole black pepper
1 tbsp crushed garlic
1 tbsp grated fresh ginger
1 tbsp salt
1 litre water

Method:
1. Sauté onions in oil with the cardamom, mustard seeds, cloves, cinnamon, red chilli, curry leaves and whole black pepper.
2. When onions turn colour add the spices: turmeric powder, chilli powder, coriander powder, cumin powder, together with the tomatoes and cook for 1min. Add ginger garlic and shallot and cook for another min.
3. Add pre-soaked Haleem mix (soup mix) and cook for 1 hour after adding a litre of water. Bring to boil and lower heat and cook till tender.
4. Add vegetables and cook for a further 30min.
5. Add coriander leaves and mint leaves 2 minutes before serving.
6. Serve hot with bread or Naan. Some people prefer to add a squeeze of lemon juice before eating.

Paapri and Methi Mootia – Indian Potato Runner Beans with Fenugreek Herb Dumplings – Gujrathi –Indian

Preparation Time: 30 min
Cooking time: 30 min
Serves: 6

Ingredients:
500g paapri (sem) beans cleaned and sliced
3 potatoes, peeled and cubed
1 large onion, chopped
1 tomato, chopped
¼ cup cooking oil
1 tsp cumin seeds
1 stick of cinnamon
2 cardamom pods
2 cloves
1 tsp chilli powder
1 tsp turmeric powder
1 tsp coriander powder
1tsp crushed garlic
1 tsp grated fresh ginger
1 cup water
1 tsp salt

Paapri and Methi Mootia (continued)

Method:
1. In a large pot sauté the onions in the oil adding, cloves, cardamom, and cumin seeds.
2. When onions begin to turn brown, add chilli powder, turmeric powder, coriander powder, garlic, ginger and tomatoes and for 1min.
3. Cook for 15min.
4. Add potatoes and salt. Layer with Mootia (dumplings).
5. Lower heat and cook till dumplings are double the size.
6. Serve with Roti or Naan.

Mootia (Dumplings)
Ingredients:

1 cup cake flour
½ cup chick pea flour
2 tsp baking powder
1 tsp salt
½ cup fenugreek (Methi) herbs, chopped
½ tsp chopped green chillies
½ tsp cumin powder
½ tsp coriander powder
2 tbsp ghee
¾ cup water

Method:
1. Sift flour salt, cumin powder, coriander powder, and baking powder together.
2. Add all other ingredients and make a dough.
3. Using wet hands drop small equal size lumps onto the beans.

Curried Green Beans and Potatoes

Preparation Time: 15 min
Cooking Time: 20 min
Serves: 4 to 6

Ingredients:
450g sliced green beans
2 medium potatoes (cleaned cut and cubed)
1 onion finely chopped
1 tsp cumin seeds
1 stick cinnamon
2 cloves
2 cardamom pods
½ tsp chilli powder
½ tsp turmeric powder
1 tsp grated fresh ginger
1 tsp crushed garlic
1tsp salt
1 small tomato, chopped
2 tablespoons ghee (melted butter)
½ cup water

Method:
1. Sauté onions in ghee adding cumin seeds, cinnamon, cloves and cardamom until onions brown a little.
2. Add turmeric powder, chilli powder, ginger, garlic salt and tomatoes and cook for 2 min.
3. Add green beans, potatoes and water and bring to boil. Lower heat and simmer till water dries out or until potatoes are tender. If more water is required, add some.
4. Serve with crusty bread or roti.

Soya Mince Curry with Potatoes

Preparation Time: 15 min
Cooking Time: 20 min
Serves: 4 to 6

Ingredients:
1 cup dry soya mince (pre-soaked overnight) or 2 cups Fry's soya mince.
4 medium potatoes, peeled and diced
1 large onion, chopped
1 tomato, chopped
1 stick cinnamon
2 cloves
2 pods cardamom
1 tsp cumin seeds
1 tsp grated fresh ginger
1 tsp crushed garlic
1 tsp cumin powder
1 tsp coriander powder
1 tsp chilli powder
1 tsp turmeric powder
1 tsp salt
4 tablespoon ghee or oil
1 cup water

Method
1. Sauté onions in ghee or oil. Add cumin seeds, cinnamon, cloves and cardamom and stir.
2. When onions are pale brown add chilli powder, turmeric powder, coriander powder, cumin powder, ginger and garlic and stir for 1 min.
3. Add tomatoes, salt, mince, potatoes and water and bring to boil. Lower heat, add curry leaves and cook till potatoes are cooked and very little is left. If you use Fry's mince cook potatoes for 10 minutes before adding mince. This mince takes less time to cook.
4. Serve with roti or rice.

Stuffed Marrow or Calabash

Preparation Time: 30 min
Cooking Time: 30 min
Serves 4 to 6

Ingredients:
1 cup Frys' Soya mince
½ cup water
1 cup chopped mixed vegetables
1 onion chopped
1 tsp curry leaves (chopped)
1 tbsp ghee
2 tbsp cooking oil
½ tsp cumin seeds
2 cinnamon sticks
2 cloves
2 tbsp tomato paste
3 cardamom pods (split open)
1 tsp cumin powder
1 tsp coriander powder
1tsp chillie powder
½ tsp turmeric powder
2 tbsp butter
Piece of string to bind marrow

Method:
1. Peel calabash or marrow. Split on one side and remove seeds.
2. Braise onion in oil and ghee adding cinnamon, cloves and cumin seeds.
3. Add all other spices together with the curry leaves and tomato paste. Cook for a minute and then add mince or vegetables. Fry for a minute.
4. Add water and cook till vegetables are cooked and water has dried out.
5. Try to prize open the slit side of marrow or calabash. Fill with vegetables or soya mince. Tie with a string to secure.
6. Rub outside with butter and bake in a preheated oven in a loaf tin or other oven proof dish for 30 minutes or until outer surface has browned.
7. Serve with roti, naan or rice.

Dhal Dhun and Katyoo (Boongee Kitchree) –Gujrathi

A complete Guajarati vegetarian meal---with rice and lentils
Preparation Time: 45 min
Cooking Time: 30 min
Serves: 6

Ingredients:
2 cups rice
2 cups toovar dhal (split pigeon peas)
1 large onion chopped fine
2 peeled chopped tomatoes
¼ cup ghee
1 tsp cumin powder
1 tsp coriander powder
1 tsp grated fresh ginger
1 tsp crushed garlic
1 tsp cumin seeds
2 cinnamon sticks
4 pods cardamom
4 cloves
1tsp salt
1 cup water

SAUCE:
Ingredients:
3 tbsp tamarind, soaked in 1cup water
2 tbsp sugar
¼ tsp mustard seeds
½ tsp cumin seeds
1 tbsp ghee
1 tbsp chick pea flour
½ tsp salt

Method:
1. Boil the rice till it is a little under done (cooked but still hard).Pass cold water through to cool and set aside.
2. Oil dhal in boiling water for 10 min .Wash in hot water several times before boiling. The dhal should be cooked but not smashed. Drain liquid into a bowl and set aside and set aside the dhal.
3. In a large pan, sauté the onions ,adding cardamom, cloves cinnamon and cumin seeds till onions turn golden brown. Now add spices, ginger, garlic, and salt .Cook for 1min.Add the dhal and cook for another min.
4. Place fried potatoes on the dhal. Cover evenly with rice .Pour 1 cup of water over the rice, cover and cook on low heat until rice is cooked soft.
5. Serve with katyoo (sauce).

Katyoo: Sauce
Method:
1. Sauté onions in ghee adding mustard seeds and cumin seeds.
2. Use your hands to separate tamarind flesh from seeds. Strain liquid and add to liquid from boiled dhal.
3. Add all the liquid into pot of sautéed onions. Add sugar chick pea flour and salt .Mix well.
4. Heat and bring to boil. Cook till sauce thickens.

Khurdi and Kitchree - Gujrathi

Ingredients for Khurdi:
1 clove garlic
1 green chilli, chopped
½ cup chopped fresh coriander leaves
1 stem curry leaves, chopped
1 small onion, chopped
2 tbsp chick pea flour
2 cups sour milk or buttermilk
1 tsp turmeric powder
1 tsp cumin seeds
½ tsp salt
3 tbsp ghee

Method:
1. Pound together coriander leaves, garlic, curry leaves and green chillies.
2. Sauté onions in ghee together with the cumin seeds, till onions soften.
3. Combine all other ingredients and add to onions.
4. Bring to boil stirring all the time till sauce thickens.
5. Serve with kitchree.

Kitchree

Ingredients:
½ cup oil dhal
2 cups rice, washed
½ cup ghee
1 small onion, chopped fine
1 tsp salt
1 tsp salt
1 tsp turmeric powder
1 tsp cumin seeds
4 cups water

Method:
1. Wash oil dhal thoroughly. In a large pot boil dhal till it is soft.
2. Sauté onion in ghee adding cumin seeds and turmeric powder. Cook till onions just about turns pale brown.
3. Add rice and cook for 1 min.
4. Add oil dhal and water and cook till rice is cooked very soft. Serve with khurdi and aloo fry (fried potatoes).

Fried Debra Calabash Patties

Preparation Time: 20 min
Cooking Time: 30 min
Serves 4 to 6

Ingredients:
1 calabash (medium size) (grated)
1 cup gram (chick pea) flour
½ cup cake flour
1 tsp baking powder
1 tsp salt
1 tsp coriander powder
1 tsp cumin powder
1 tsp chillie powder
1 tsp chopped green chillies
½ cup chopped coriander leaves
1 onion chopped
1 tsp garlic paste
Oil for shallow frying

Method:
1. Peel calabash with a potato peeler. Remove seeds and grate.
2. Add all ingredients and make a very thick batter. Do not add water. Make equal size balls and flatten in the palm of the hand.
3. In a non-stick pan fry the "patties" till brown on either side.
4. Serve as a starter or savoury snack with a sauce or dip of your choice.

Dhai Waras (Sweet)

Preparation Time: 20 min
Cooking Time: 30 min
Serves 4 to 6

Ingredients:
2 cups flour plus flour for rolling and cutting
2 tsp baking powder
1 tsp jeera (cumin) seeds
2 tbsp ghee

Syrup:
2 cups sugar
1 cup water
½ tsp elachi powder (cardamom). (Prepare by boiling for 10 min) set aside to cook.

Method:
1. Soak cumin seeds in ¼ cup boiling water.
2. Sift flour and baking powder.
3. Rub in ghee.
4. Make a soft dough using the maas.
5. Roll out dough on a well-floured board. Cut into shapes.
6. Deep fry until golden brown.
7. Dunk into syrup while still hot. Remove from syrup into a colander.
8. Serve as a dessert or teatime treat.

Phirni -- Rice and Milk Pudding

Preparation Time: 10 min
Cooking Time: 15 min
Serves 4 to 6

Ingredients:
1 litre milk
2 tbsp rice flour, coarsely ground
¼ tsp elachi powder if prepared
2 tbsp ghee
¼ cup sugar
¼ cup ground almonds
1 drop of pink food colouring
Some slivered almonds

Method:
1. Fry rice flour in ghee till it turns colour slightly.
2. Add milk, elachi powder, food colouring, almond powder and sugar
3. Heat and bring to boil stirring all the time, till mixture thickens.
4. Pour into individual serving bowls or in one large bowl. Place in refrigerator to cool.
5. Garnish with slivered almonds and serve as a desert.

Ghor Papri -- (Naani's Recipe)

Preparation Time: 10 min
Cooking Time: 30 min
Serves 4 to 6

Ingredients:
500g ghor (Ghur or Jaggery)
500g ghee
¼ cup semolina
2 tsp elaachi (cardamom) powder
1 cup ground almonds
500g brown bread flour
½ cup milk

Method:
1. Fry brown flour in the ghee till a distinct colour change and an aroma is noticeable.
2. Add Ghur, elaachi and ground almonds and milk.
3. The jaggery will melt into the mixture but will not bind until packed hard into a swiss roll tray.
4. Press down hard, flatten evenly and allow to cool. Cut into squares before it turns hard.
5. Serve as a sweetmeat.

Baklava

Preparation Time: 15 min
Cooking Time: 20 min
Serves 4 to 6

Ingredients:
1 cup ghee
6 sheets of phlylo pastry
1 cup ground nuts
1 cup slivered nuts (cashews, hazel, almonds and pistachio)
3 tbsp honey
¼ cup chopped dates
Castor sugar for sprinkling on top

Method:
1. Mix all nuts, honey and dates.
2. In a greased baking sheet place 1 sheet of phylo pastry which has been greased on both sides.
3. Divide nuts mixture into five portions.
4. Sprinkle one portion evenly on the first sheet.
5. Grease the second sheet on both sides and place over the mixture on the 1st sheet. Repeat till all sheets and mixture is finished.
6. Cover top sheet and allow baking tray to stand in a refrigerator for 20 minutes. When cool use a sharp knife and cut pastry into portion sized squares or diamond shapes
7. Bake in a preheated oven (200^0C) for 30 minutes until Baklava is golden brown colour.
8. Remove from oven and sprinkle castor sugar generously while hot. Allow to cool, serve as a desert with tea.

Plain Soji Halwa

Preparation Time: 10 min
Cooking Time: 15 min
Serves 4 to 6

Ingredients:
1 cup tasty wheat or semolina
½ cup ghee
¼ cup cooking oil
500ml milk
⅓ cup sugar
2 cinnamon sticks
1 teaspoon cardamom powder
½ cup slivered almonds

Method:
1. Fry semolina in ghee and oil stirring all the time till the semolina turns light brown. Add cinnamon sticks and elaachi (cardamom) powder. Fry for 5 minutes.
2. Add sugar and milk. Stir lower heat and cover pot. Cook stirring every now and then till all the water is absorbed.
3. Stir till the mixture leaves the sides of the pot and the "ghee" is visible.
4. The halwas are ready. Serve garnished with slivered almonds.

Carrot Halwa

Preparation Time: 20 min
Cooking Time: 30 min
Serves 4 to 6

Ingredients:
3 cups carrot pulp
2 litres milk
½ cup ghee
½ cup sugar
½ cup ground almonds
2 tsp elaachi (cardamom) powder
3 tbsp coloured almonds for garnishing

Method:
1. Boil carrot pulp in milk till cooked.
2. Add ghee, sugar, ground almonds and elaachi and allow to cook on low heat till the "halwa" comes away from the sides of the pot.
3. Serve hot, garnished with coloured almonds, with whipped fresh cream or condensed cream as a desert.

Puff Pastry Jam Turn Overs

Preparation Time: 20 min
Cooking Time: 30 min
Serves 4 to 6

1 puff pastry makes 12 small turnovers like the shape of sausage rolls.
Diagram on how to cut the pastry.

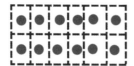

Ingredients:
1 puff pastry
2 tbsp flour to make a paste.
Sugar to sprinkle on top
Some jam of your choice
Some oil to brush on top

Method:
1. Preheat oven to 200^{0}C
2. Make a paste of flour and water and brush on entire surface of pastry.
3. Divide pastry by cutting as above.
4. Place a teaspoon of jam on each centre. Turn each end onto the centre. Press sides and place on a baking tray with the open end at the bottom.
5. Brush cooking oil on top and carefully sprinkle some sugar on the oily surface.
6. Bake in preheated oven till the pastry is well risen and a golden brown in colour.

Egyptian Ducca and Morrocan Sprinkle

Ingredients:
1 tsp crushed coriander
1 tsp jeera powder
2 tsp turmeric powder
1 tsp crushed red chillies
½ cup ground almonds and cashew nuts
½ tsp crushed black pepper
1 tsp roasted crushed garlic
1 tsp ground ginger
½ tsp nutmeg powder
½ tsp cardamom powder

Method:
1. Mix all ingredients together in a glass jar. Use as a sprinkle on baked vegetables, pasta or any savoury dish when desired. It is a delicious additive to enhance the flavours of the dish made.

Dhal for filling: Milti Roti

Preparation Time: 30 min
Cooking Time: 30 min
Serves 4 to 6

Ingredients:
2 cups oil Dhal (Joovar Dhal)
2 cups water
1 tsp elaachi powder
1 cup sugar
2 tbsp ghee

Dough:
2 cups flour
3 tbsp ghee
½ tsp salt
2 tbsp sugar
About 1½ cups boiling water

Method:
A) Dhal Filling
1. Soak dhal in boiling water for 1 hour. Wash thoroughly to remove oil. Boil till soft and mushy.
2. Add sugar and ghee and cook till sugar dissolves and dhal gets dry.
3. Add elaachi (cardamom) powder and allow to cool.

B) Dough
1. Mix flour, sugar and salt. Rub in ghee. Pour boiling water into flour and mix quickly. Allow to cool and knead into a soft dough.
2. Make equal sized ball, roll small rounds. Make equal rounds of dhal and place 1 ball in centre of round roti. Cover into a parcel, resembling a ball. The dough should cover the dhal ball with the joined part at the bottom.
3. Place the ball on a floured board and roll flat rounds as gently as you can. Do not allow filling to come out. The now "filled" roti is ready to cook.
4. On a griddle pan or non-stick pan cook the roti on each side brushing with ghee on each side till roti dough is specked and cooked. Place on wire rack to cool.
NB. This is a gujrathi dish served with tea as a snack. A similar savoury dish can be made with mashed potatoes, sweet potatoes or other dhalls or lentils, flavourings with dhanya and green chillies. The above dhal filling can also be used in samoosas or tarts using puff pastry.

Vegetable Breyani

Preparation Time: 1 hour
Cooking Time: 35 min
Serves: 6

Ingredients:
3 cups Basmati rice
500g frozen or fresh vegetables of choice
½ cup black lentils (Masoor)
3 large potatoes, peeled and quartered'
2 large onions, chopped
2 tomatoes peeled and chopped
½ cup ghee
2 whole green chillies
1 sprig curry leaves
½ cup chopped coriander leaves
1 cup yogurt
1 tbsp crushed garlic
1 tbsp grated fresh ginger
1 tbsp salt
1 tsp cumin seeds
2 sticks cinnamon
4 cloves
4 pods cardamom
1 tsp chilli powder
1 tsp turmeric powder
1 tsp coriander powder
1tsp cumin powder
Oil to fry potatoes
1 cup water

Vegatable Breyani (continued)

Method:
1. Combine ginger, garlic, green chilli, curry leaves, salt, cumin powder, coriander powder, turmeric powder, chilli powder, tomatoes and yogurt in a bowl. Add vegetables and allow to marinate.
2. Fry potatoes till they are pale brown in colour. Set aside.
3. Boil rice till it is slightly under done. Set aside.
4. Boil lentils till cooked. Set aside.
5. Set 1tbsp of onion. Sauté the rest of the onions in the ghee adding cumin seeds, cinnamon, cloves, and cardamom. Fry onions till golden brown. Remove onion and spices from ghee and mix into vegetables.
6. Spread 1cup of cooked rice at the bottom of pot in which onions were fried. The ghee should still be there.
7. Spread vegetables on the rice.
8. Spread potatoes on top of the vegetables evenly.
9. Cover the potatoes with the lentils.
10. Lastly pour the rest of the rice over the lentils.
11. Drizzle the water over the rice.
12. Preheat oven to 160 ° C.
13. Heat pot on top of cooker for 5min. You will hear the sound of cooking in the pot.
14. In a pan, using a little ghee, fry the balance of the onions till light brown. Spread over the rice.
15. Place pot into oven and allow to steam for 30 min.
16. Serve as a complete dish with a yogurt salad.

Yogurt Salad

Ingredients:
1 chopped onion
1 green chilli
1 clove crushed garlic.
2 tbsp fresh coriander leaves, finely chopped
1 cucumber, finely chopped
2 cups yogurt
½ tsp salt
½ tsp freshly ground black pepper

Method:
Mix all ingredients together and serve with Breyani

Cauliflower Potatoes and Peas cooked in Yogurt

Preparation Time: 30 min
Cooking Time: 30 min
Serves: 6

Ingredients:
2 large potatoes, peeled and cut into cubes
Oil for deep frying
1 medium cauliflower, cut into florets
1 large onion, finely chopped
1 cup frozen peas
1 tsp chopped green chillies or crushed red chillies
1 tsp crushed garlic
½ tsp turmeric powder
½ tsp coarsely ground black pepper
1 tsp salt
1 cup plain yogurt or sour cream
1 tbsp fresh chopped coriander

Method:
1. In a wok pour enough oil and fry potatoes until golden brown. Remove potatoes and set aside.
2. Now fry the cauliflower till tender but still firm. Remove from oil and set aside.
3. Fry peas for 5min. Remove and set aside.
4. Sauté onions in ghee till soft. Add salt, pepper, garlic, chillies and turmeric powder into the ghee and fry for 1min. Add vegetables.
5. Pour yogurt and cook for 5min.
6. Garnish with coriander and with rice.

Curried Zucchini Green Peppers and Tomatoes

Preparation Time: 30 min
Cooking Time: 15 min
Serves: 4 to 6

Ingredients:
2 Tbsp ghee
1 large onion, chopped
1 tsp crushed garlic
1 tsp grated fresh ginger
1 tsp cumin seeds
1tsp green chillies, chopped
1 tsp turmeric powder
2 small green peppers, cleaned and diced
6 medium zucchinis cut into cubes
6 medium tomatoes peeled and cut
1 tsp salt
1 tsp sugar
1 tbsp fresh coriander to garnish

Method:
1. In a wok sauté onions adding the cumin seeds.
2. When onions are soft, add ginger, garlic, green chillies, salt, turmeric powder, and ground coriander and stir for 1min.
3. Add zucchinis and cook for 5min.
4. Add peppers and cook for 5min.
5. Lastly add tomatoes and sugar and cook for a further 2min.
6. Garnish with coriander and serve with rice or roti.

Stir Fried Vegetables with Soya Strips

Preparation Time: 40 min
Cooking Time: 10 min
Serves: 6

Ingredients:
4 tbsp olive oil
1 chopped onion
450g soya strips (Fry's)
450g stir fry vegetables
 Marinade for vegetables:
2 tbsp Maggie Worcestershire sauce
2 tbsp brown sugar
¼ cup brown vinegar
1tsp salt
¼ tsp freshly ground black pepper
1 tbsp crunchy peanut butter
1 tsp Dijon mustard
1 tsp crushed garlic
1 tsp crushed garlic
1 tsp chopped green chillies

Method:
1. Combine all marinade ingredients and marinade vegetables in the marinade for 30 min.
2. Sauté onions in olive oil until onions turn colour. Add vegetables and stir fry till vegetables are cooked but still crunchy.
3. Add soya strips and stir for 5min. Cover and cook for another 5min.
4. Serve with fluffy white rice or noodles.

British Type Roasted Tomato Soup

Preparation Time: 30 min
Cooking Time: 45 min
Serves: 6

Ingredients:
1.5kg ripe tomatoes
4 cloves garlic, peeled and chopped
$^1/_3$ cup olive oil
1 tbsp mixed dried herbs
1 tbsp salt
½ tsp freshly ground black pepper
1 cup water
¼ cup red wine vinegar
3 tsp sugar

Method:
NB---it would be advisable to prepare early
1. Preheat oven to 160 °C
2. Rinse tomatoes and cut in half. Coat with garlic herbs and olive oil.
3. Roast in oven for 45min. Remove and cool.
4. Process in food processor until smooth.
5. Add all other ingredients and mix. If you want to adjust seasoning, do so. Add water to get desired consistency and chill for at least 6 for hours for flavours to develop.

Summer Lettuce and Pea Soup

Preparation Time: 30min
Cooking time: 15min
Serves: 6

Ingredients:
125g butter
1 iceberg lettuce washed and sliced into strips.
500g baby peas
2 tsp salt
½ tsp crushed black pepper
1tsp salt
1 litre boiling water
Fresh mint

Method:
1. Melt butter in a large sauce pan. Put aside a little lettuce mint and peas for garnishing and add the rest together with salt and sugar and black pepper and cook for 5min.
2. Add water and cook till peas are tender for about 5 min. cool, puree in a blender or pass through a sieve.
3. Return to pan, reheat and serve. Garnish with lettuce peas and mint.
4. You can even serve it cold. Just chill in refrigerator.

Potato Salad

Preparation Time: 10 min
Cooking time: 20 min
Serves: 6

Ingredients:
6 fat spring onions, chopped
1 cup cream cheese
½ cup yogurt
1 tsp chopped dill or mint
700 g baby or new potatoes

Method:
1. Sprinkle some salt on the spring onions and allow to stand for 20min.
2. Boil potatoes till cooked. Remove from pot and put into serving dish.
3. Combine cream cheese, yogurt, pepper, dill or mint, and rinsed onions.
4. Chop potatoes with a knife to break them up .Add yogurt dressing while still warm.
5. Serve with 'sausages' or patties or 'meat loaf' made of soya.

Butternut Caramelised in Honey

Preparation Time: 10 min
Cooking time: 30 min
Serves: 6

Ingredients:
1 butternut, cleaned and cubed
1 tbsp olive oil
100ml honey
1 tsp crushed garlic
1 tsp cinnamon powder
1 tsp chopped fresh thyme
1 tbsp butter
¼ cup water

Method:
1. Preheat oven to 180 ° C.
2. Mix all ingredients in a large dish and toss butternut in the mix.
3. Place on prepared baking sheet and bake until the butternut is soft and caramelized, about 30min.

Double Mushroom Burger

Preparation Time: 20 min
Cooking Time: 25 min
Serves: 6

Ingredients:
large brown mushrooms
40ml butter
1 large onion, finely chopped
1 cup canned chick peas, drained
½ cup low fat cottage cheese
6 tomato slices
¼ cup crumbed blue cheese
6 lettuce leaves, curly or iceberg
Chopped chives to garnish

Method:
1. Remove stalks and chop them fine.
2. Heat ½ the butter in a pan and fry the mushrooms on both sides. Set aside.
3. In the same pan use using the rest of the butter fry onions, chick peas and mushroom stalks till stalks are soft for about 2 to 3 min. Remove from heat.
4. Place 6 of the mushrooms in a baking tray. Spoon chick pea filling into each one. Spread cottage cheese onto the chick pea and top each with a tomato, season with salt and pepper.
5. Place the remaining 6 mushrooms and sprinkle blue cheese on top. Bake in preheated oven for 10min until blue cheese melts.
6. Remove from oven. Lift the top mushroom and place a lettuce leaf into each of the burgers. Garnish with chopped chives.

Meat Loaf Using Soya Mince

Preparation Time: 20 min
Cooking Time: 30 min
Serves: 4 to 6

Ingredients:
½ cup dry soya mince or 1 packet Fry's soya mince.
1 potatoes, boiled and mashed
1 large onion, chopped fine
1 teaspoon salt
½ teaspoon crushed black pepper
1 tablespoon Maggi Worcestershire sauce
1 tablespoon finely chopped shallot leaves
1 tablespoon chopped fresh parsley
1 teaspoon thyme
½ teaspoon cinnamon powder
3 tablespoons flour
3 tablespoons tomato paste
2 tablespoons butter
1 teaspoon crushed fresh ginger
1 teaspoon crushed garlic
1 cup water

Method:
1. Dry soya mince has to be pre-soaked for 15min by pouring boiling water over it and allowing it to stand so as to re hydrate .Fry's soya mince does not need soaking.
2. Preheat oven to 180^{0}F
3. In a pan sauté the onions in the butter.
4. Add ginger and garlic, tomato paste, salt, pepper and Worcestershire sauce. Fry mince for 5min. Add water and cook for 10min if you use dry soya mince. Set aside to cool.
5. In a mixing bowl, combine all ingredients and mix thoroughly.
6. Place in a greased loaf tin and bake in prepared oven for 30 min. or until skewer comes clean.
6. Serve with vegetables or a salad.

Soya Mince - Shepherds Pie

Preparation Time: 15 min
Cooking Time: 30 min
Serves: 4 to 6

Ingredients:
500g soya mince
3 potatoes peeled and cubed
2 tsp salt
1 large onion chopped
1 tsp crushed garlic
1 tsp freshly grated ginger
½ tsp freshly grated black pepper.
1 tbsp chopped fresh parsley
1 tbsp chopped fresh thyme
2 tbsp Worcester sauce
1 chopped tomato
125g butter
Water for boiling

Method:
1. Boil potatoes in water with 1tsp salt .Mash potatoes add butter and mix. Set aside.
2. Sauté onions in oil. Add tomatoes, garlic, ginger, salt, pepper, Worcester sauce and herbs.
3. Add mince and cook for 5min. Add ½ cup water.
4. Spoon mince into a greased casserole dish. Spread evenly.
5. Spread mash over the mince very evenly. Garnish with parsley. Serve hot.

SAUCES

A. White Sauce

Ingredients:
2 tbsp butter
2 tbsp flour
1 cup milk
1 tsp salt
½ tsp freshly ground black pepper
1 tbsp chopped parsley or thyme

Method:
1. Heat butter in a sauce pan. Lower heat and add flour. Stir all the time and fry flour in butter it starts to turn colour. While still pale add milk and bring to boil stirring all the time till sauce thickens.
2. Add salt and pepper and herbs.
3. Use for pasta or vegetables like potatoes, cabbage, cauliflower and brussels sprouts.

B. Cheese Sauce

Method:
1. Make above sauce. When slightly cool add grated cheddar cheese and stir vigorously until mixed.
2. Use for pasta.
3. Add 1 tbsp of Dijon mustard and mix.
4. Use on boiled carrots, parsnips and burgers. This sauce can also be used soya prawns and soya fish licks

DRESSINGS

Dressing for Steamed Brocolli Cabbage or Cauliflower

Ingredients:
¼ cup balsamic vinegar
2 tbsp olive oil
1 tbsp Dijon mustard
1tbsp lemon juice
Herbs of choice
Salt and pepper

Method:
Mix all ingredients and pour over vegetables. Mix and serve.

Salad Dressing

Ingredients:
1 tbsp mayonnaise
1 tbsp Dijon mustard
1 tbsp olive oil
1 tbsp lemon juice
1 tsp crushed garlic
½ tsp salt
½ tsp freshly ground black pepper

Method:
Mix all ingredients, pour over salad and toss

Tartare Sauce

Ingredients:
3 tbsp lemon juice
3 tbsp lime juice
1 tsp Dijon mustard
2 tbsp olive oil
2 tbsp sugar or honey
1 tbsp fresh dill, chopped
1 tbsp fresh basil, chopped
Salt and black pepper to taste
1 tsp crushed garlic

Method:
Mix all ingredients together.
Use for soya chicken soy prawns and soya burgers.

Dressing for Roasted Vegetable Salad

Add 2 tbsp mayonnaise to above sauce and pour over vegetables before roasting.

DIP – STARTERS - MIDDLE EASTERN STYLE

Tahini Dip

Preparation Time: 10 min
Cooking Time: 10 min
Serves: 4 to 6

Ingredients
12 cloves garlic
2 tablespoon ground cumin
1 tsp grated lemon rind
2/3 cup Tahini paste (sesame seed paste)
½ cup lemon juice
½ cup water

Method:
1. Peel garlic. Bake in a hot oven for 10 min till soft.
2. Blend all ingredients adding juice and water a little at a time till well blended.
3. Serve with crackers or toasted tortillas.
Please use vegetable oil to cook because sesame oil has a very strong flavour. Sesame oil should be used more for flavouring rather than cooking.

Broad Bean Dip

Preparation Time: 10 min
Cooking Time: 10 min
Serves: 4 to 6

Ingredients
½ cup olive oil
1 medium onion, finely chopped
1 clove crushed garlic
1 tsp ground cumin
500g frozen or tinned broad beans
¾ cup water
1 tbsp lemon juice
1 tbsp chopped parsley or coriander leaves

Method:
1. Using 2 tablespoon of oil in a pan sauté the onions till soft. Add beans and cook for 5min. Add spices and lemon juice.
2. Blend till smooth.
3. Return beans to pan and cook for 5min till heated.
4. Add herb of choice and stir.
5. Serve with bread sticks or vegetable sticks.

Baba Ghanoush---(Brinjal or Egg Plant Dip)

Ingredients:
2 large (1kg) egg plants (brinjal)
½ cup plain yogurt
2 tbsp lemon juice
2cloves garlic, crushed
¼ cup tahini paste (sesame paste)
2 tsp ground cumin
½ cup fresh coriander leaves

Method:
1. Pierce egg plants all over with a sharp knife. Place whole egg plants on a baking tray. Bake uncovered in a very hot oven for about an hour. Allow to cool.
2. Skin egg plants and chop up the flesh.
3. Using a blender, process adding remaining ingredients until well mixed.
4. Sprinkle with chopped parsley and serve with pita bread or crackers.

Hummus ----Chick Pea Dip

Ingredients:
2 tbsp olive oil
1 medium onion, chopped
4 cloves garlic, crushed
2 tsp cumin powder
2 tins (250g) chick peas
½ cup tahini paste
½ cup lemon juice
1 tbsp fresh chopped coriander leaves
1 tsp chilli powder
¾ cup buttermilk

Method:
1. Heat oil in pan, add onion and garlic and cook till onion is soft. Add cumin powder and stir till fragrant. Cool and set aside.
2. Blend or process chick peas, tahini, lemon juice, coriander, paprika, buttermilk and onion mixture until smooth.
3. Spoon into serving bowl .drizzle with a little olive oil and garnish with coriander leaves.
4. Serve with crackers or crusty bread.

Red Pepper Dip

Ingredients:
1 large red pepper
250g fat free plain smooth cottage cheese
2 tbsp balsamic vinegar
2 tsp cumin powder
1 small red chilli, deseeded and chopped
1 tsp salt
¼ tsp freshly ground black pepper

Method:
1. Halve and deseed pepper and place under grill until skin turns black.
2. Cool and remove skin.
3. Put all ingredients into a blender and process till smooth.
4. Serve with crackers or crusty bread.

Creamy Watercress and Pear Dip

Ingredients:
100 g leeks, washed and chopped
200g potatoes, peeled and chopped
30 g butter
100ml vegetable stock
1 tin canned pears
75ml fresh cream
50 g cream cheese
1 tsp salt
½ tsp freshly crushed black pepper

Method:
1. Sauté leeks and potato in butter for 5min on low heat.
2. Add stock and cook until potatoes are soft. (about 20min)
3. Add watercress, pears and cream cheese. Blend until smooth.
4. Garnish with grated cheese and serve crusty bread or crackers.

Mango and Coriander Dip or Salsa

Ingredients: FOR KEY RECIPE
2 large mangoes and 2 tbsp salt
1 bunch fresh coriander leaves
1 chopped green chilli
2 cloves garlic, crushed
1 tsp salt
½ tsp freshly ground black pepper
2 tbsp olive oil

Method:
1. Clean and chop mango. Cover with salt and allow to stand for 2 hours. The salt draws the natural liquid out of the fruit.
2. In a food processor process coriander, garlic and green chilli. Add salt and pepper and olive and mix.
3. Rinse and drain mango. Use a kitchen towel to remove excess liquid. Place into processor and process with other ingredients.
4. Pour into serving bowl and garnish with coriander leaves.

Apple and Coriander---Pineapple and Coriander---Sweet Mango and Coriander

All of the above are made the same way as green mango and coriander dip.

Avocado and Coriander

This fruit does not need salting. Instead, add ¼ cup of lemon juice and mix.

Peanut Butter, Coriander and Mint Dip

To the key recipe
1. Leave out the fruit.
2. Add ½ cup lemon juice.
3. Add ½ cup fresh mint.
4. Mix well.

Date and Coriander Dip

Ingredients:
250g seedless dates
½ cup vinegar
2 tsp crushed garlic
1 tsp cumin powder
¼ cup lemon juice
2 bunches of fresh coriander
1 tsp salt

Method:
1. Pound together or liquidise green chillies, coriander, garlic and lemon juice.
2. Boil vinegar and dates. Cool.
3. Combine all ingredients and mix well. Bottle and refrigerate. Use when desired as a dip relish or sauce.

BAKING

Milk Scones

Preparation Time: 15 min
Baking time: 20 min
Makes: 6 large scones

Ingredients:
2 cups cake flour
4 teaspoons baking powder
2 tbsp butter or margarine
¾ cup milk
½ tsp salt
3 tbsp sugar

Method:
1. Preheat oven to 220° C.
2. Sift flour, salt, and baking powder together.
3. Add butter and sugar and rub together until mixture resembles bread crumbs.
4. Add milk and stir, using a fork, till mixture becomes like soft dough.
5. Turn onto a floured board and toss until smooth. Pat flat to about 20 to 25 mm thick. Using a cutter cut into rounds.
6. Brush with oil and bake on a baking sheet for 15 to 20 min.
7. Cool on wire rack and serve with butter and jam.

Griddle Scones

Preparation Time: 10 min
Cooking Time: 20 min

Ingredients
2 cups flour
4 teaspoons baking powder
1 cup milk
1 tsp cream of tarter
1 tsp salt
1 tsp golden syrup or honey
3 tsp hot water

Method:
1. Sieve all dry ingredients.
2. Dissolve syrup with hot water .Add to milk.
3. Using a fork, mix everything together. Mixture will become a soft dough.
4. Roll on a floured board, pat flat to about 10mm thick. Cut into rounds or triangles and cook on a greased griddle pan until they brown on each side. Pan temperature must not be too high.
5. Serve with butter and jam or fresh cream and jam.

Cheese and Herb Scones

Preparation Time: 10 min
Baking Time: 15 min
Makes: 12

Ingredients:
3 cups flour
6 tsp baking powder
1 tsp salt
1 tsp mixed dried herbs
3 tbsp sugar
1 cup grated cheddar cheese.
1 tsp chopped shallot leaves
½ tsp grated fresh black pepper
2 cups Maas or yogurt
½ cup oil or butter

Method:
Preheat oven to 200° C
1. Sift together flour, baking powder and salt.
2. Rub oil into the flour mixture and blend until mixture resembles fine bread crumbs.
3. Add sugar and blend again.
4. Add cheese and blend.
5. At this stage one can change the recipe. Instead of adding cheese, herbs and black pepper add:
    a) 1 tbsp poppy seeds and 1 tsp orange essence or
    b) 1 tbsp lemon zest and 1 tsp lemon essence or
    c) ½ cup currants and 1tsp vanilla essence.
6. Using a fork mix yogurt into flour mixture until a soft dough forms.
7. Roll out on a floured board and cut into rounds.
8. Brush cooking oil on top of scones and bake till golden brown for about 20min.
9. Brush with oil again while still hot. This prevents drying.
10 Serve either with butter and cheese or with jam and cream.

Cup Cakes ---Poppy Seed and Orange

Preparation Time; 15 min
Baking time: 25 min
Makes: 2 trays, medium

Ingredients:
½ cup sugar
¾ cup oil
3 cups cake flour
3 tsp baking powder
1 tsp orange essence
1 tbsp black poppy seeds
1½ cups milk

Method:
1. Preheat oven to 180 ° C.
2. Sift flour and baking powder together and mix.
3. Beat sugar and oil till creamy.
4. Add flour mixture, to the sugar mixture. Add poppy seeds essence and milk and beat till smooth.
5. Spoon mixture into paper cups placed in muffin trays. Till each cup is ¾ full.
6. Bake till well risen and golden brown in colour for about 20min.
7. Remove from oven and cool on wire rack.

Eggless Sponge

Preparation Time: 20 min
Baking Time: 30 min

Ingredients:
1¾ cups self raising flour.
2 tsp baking powder
1¾ cup castor sugar
6 tbsp cooking oil or melted butter
1 cup water
1 tsp vanilla essence
4 tbsp jam
Castor sugar for dusting

Method:
1. Preheat oven to 180° C.
2. Sift flour and baking powder. Stir in the castor sugar.
3. Pour oil, water and vanilla into mixture and mix well until smooth.
4. Divide and pour mixture into prepared (20cm) sandwich tins equally.
5. Bake in oven for about 25 to 30 min.
6. Allow to cool. Turn out and transfer on wire rack.
7. Spread jam on underside and make a sandwich. Sprinkle with castor sugar on top.

Chocolate Tray Bake

Preparation Time: 10 min
Baking Time 15 min
Large oven tray bake

Ingredients:
3 cups flour
4 tsp baking powder
½ tsp salt
1 tsp bicarbonate of soda
1 tsp salt
1/3 cup cocoa
2 cups sugar
1/5 cup white vinegar
1 cup cooking oil
2 cups boiling water

Method:
1. Preheat oven to 180° C.
2. Sift together flour, baking powder, salt, bicarbonate of soda and cocoa.
3. In another dish combine sugar vinegar and oil.
4. Boil the water. Combine all ingredients in the larger dish. Add boiling water and mix quickly.
5. Pour mixture into a prepared oven tray (well-greased), and bake for 15 min or until mixture begins to move away from sides of tray.
6. Spread icing while still warm. Cut into squares before serving.

Icing:
2 tbsp soft butter
1½ cups icing sugar
2 tbsp cocoa
½ tsp vanilla essence
3 tbsp warm water

Method:
Mix all ingredients together. It must be able to spread .Add more water if necessary.
Beat till smooth

Bhengori's Shortbread Fingers

Preparation time: 10 min
Baking Time; 1½ hours
Bakes: 1 tray

Ingredients:
500g butter
Icing sugar
1 cup maizena (maize flour)
4 cups flour

Method:
1. Preheat oven to 160° C.
2. Beat butter and sugar.
3. Sift flour and maizena into butter mixture. Mix to form a dough.
4. Pat into a Swiss roll tray and using a fork pierce holes into dough all over evenly.
5. Bake in a preheated oven until golden brown (about 1 to1½ hours).
6. Cut while hot but cool before removing from tray.

Chocolate Biscuits -- Like Romany Creams

Preparation time: 15 min
Baking time: 30 min
Makes: 24

Ingredients:
250 g butter
125ml boiling water
160ml coconut
Pinch of salt
60g cocoa
5ml baking powder
200g castor sugar
240g flour, maybe a little more might be required.
1 slab cooking chocolate

Method:
1. Preheat oven to 180° C.
2. Cream butter and sugar.
3. Sift flour, baking powder, salt and cocoa .Add to butter and sugar.
4. Add water and coconut. Mix adding extra flour to remove mixture from sides of bowl.
5. Place teaspoon on baking tray or use a biscuit gun.
6. Bake for 10 min.
7. When cool sandwich two together with melted chocolate.

Crunchies

Preparation time: 10 min
Baking time: 10 min
Makes: 1 tray

Ingredients:
1 cup sugar
1 cup coconut
1 cup butter or margarine
3 tsp golden syrup
1 cup flour
2 cups oats
½ tsp bicarbonate of soda
Pinch of salt

Method:
1. Preheat oven to 180°C.
2. Sift flour and bicarbonate of soda. Add all dry ingredients to it.
3. Melt butter in syrup. Add to dry ingredients .Mix well.
4. Press into a greased Swiss roll tray.
5. Bake for 10 minutes on top shelf of oven.
6. Cool before cutting.

Chocolate icing can be spread on it if desired.

Chocolate Icing

Ingredients:
1 cup icing sugar
2 tbsp butter
2 tbsp cocoa
3 tbsp warm water
½ tsp vanilla essence

Method:
Mix all ingredients together to make a runny paste. Spread quickly over cold crunchies. Cut when dry.

Date Crackers

Preparation time: 20 min
Baking Time: 30 min
Bakes: 1tray

Ingredients:
625g flour
250ml brown sugar
250ml butter
500 g stoned dates
3ml bicarbonate of soda
250 ml white sugar
125ml cold water
125ml hot water
625ml oats

Method:
1. Preheat oven to 160° C.
2. Put dates, white sugar and cold water into sauce pan. Boil until dates are soft. Allow to cool.
3. Beat butter and brown sugar. Add oats and flour, then hot water with the bicarbonate of soda. Make a dough.
4. Divide the dough into two parts. Roll out thin.
5. Spread date mixture on one part. Cover with the second biscuit like a sandwich. Cut into small squares.
6. Place squares on a baking tray and bake till they turn light brown.

Peanut Butter Biscuits

Preparation Time: 30 min
Baking Time: 30 min
Makes: about 30

Ingredients:
125 ml peanut butter
125ml brown sugar
3ml salt
125ml butter or margarine
125ml white sugar
440ml flour
3ml bicarbonate of soda
5ml baking powder
1 tbsp white vinegar

Method:
1. Pre-heat oven to 180° C.
2. Cream white sugar, brown sugar, peanut butter, margarine and vinegar.
3. Sift flour baking powder bicarbonate of soda and salt.
4. Add to creamed mixture and make a soft dough.
5. Break teaspoons of dough and make balls and place on a baking tray. Use a fork to mark each ball and flatten in the process.
6. Bake for 10 to 15 min in oven till golden brown.
7. Cool before lifting.

Chocolate Squares

Preparation Time: 45 min
Cooking Time: 10 min
Makes: 1tray.

Ingredients:
300g Milk or dark chocolate
175g margarine
30ml golden syrup
300g eggless biscuit, crushed
75g chopped pecan nuts
75g glazed cherries

Method:
1. Melt the chocolate margarine and syrup in sauce pan over low heat.
2. Remove from heat and stir in biscuits crumbs, nuts, and cherries.
3. Press into greased tray and chill until firm.

Butter Biscuits -- with Coconut, Dates Cherries and Almonds

Preparation Time: 30 min
Baking Time: 20 min per tray

Ingredients:
100g icing sugar
350g butter
5ml vanilla essence
250g flour
100g corn flour
Castor sugar for sprinkling

Method:
1. Preheat oven to 180 °C
2. Mix all ingredients to make soft dough. If dough is too soft add a little more flour.
3. Roll out on floured surface and cut out shapes.
4. If you do not want shapes roll into a long sausage shape and refrigerate for 30 min. Cut with a sharp knife into circles of equal thickness.
5. Place onto a baking sheet and bake till golden brown.
6. Remove from oven and sprinkle with castor sugar while still hot.

Variations:
1. Add 1 cup coconut before mixing dough.
2. Add ½ cup almond powder before mixing dough.
3. Add ½ cup finely chopped dates before mixing dough.
4. Add chopped glazed cherries to dough. Decorate top with a piece of cherry.

Melting Moments –Biscuits

Preparation Time: 15 min
Baking Time: 30 min
Makes: 30

Ingredients:
250g butter
60g icing sugar
180g flour (sifted)
60g maizena (sifted)
Pinch of salt

Method:
1. Preheat oven to 180° C.
2. Cream butter and sugar.
3. Sift together flour, corn flour (maizena), and salt. Gradually blend into creamed mixture. Beat well.
4. On a greased tray, using two teaspoons, drop about 10 ml amounts to make little heaps.
5. Decorate with glazed cherries by pressing the cherry in the centre to flatten biscuit.
6. Bake for 10 to 15 min until pale brown.
7. Remove from oven cool for 10 min, then loosen and cool on a wire rack.

Naan Khatai –Gujrathi Biscuit

Preparation Time: 10 min
Baking time: 30 min
Makes: 24

Ingredients:
1 cup ghee (melted clarified butter)
¾ cup cooking oil
1 tsp baking powder
¼ tsp bicarbonate of soda
¼ tsp ground nutmeg
1 tsp powdered cardamom
1 tbsp chick pea flour
3 cups flour (if dough is too soft add more)
Coloured almonds to decorate

Method:
1. Preheat oven to 180° C.
2. Beat sugar, ghee and cooking oil together.
3. Sift flour with baking powder, nutmeg, cardamom and bicarbonate of soda.
4. Add to sugar mixture and make a soft dough.
5. Make small round balls and place on a baking tray. Decorate with a coloured almond pressed on centre of each ball.
6. Bake until golden brown –about 20 min. Cool and then remove from tray.

Hungarian Tart or Crumble Tart

Preparation time: 20 min
Baking Time: 20 min

Ingredients:
250g butter or margarine
2 cups flour
2 tbsp chick pea flour
2 tsp baking powder
½ cup jam (of preference)

Method:
1. Preheat oven to 180° C.
2. Cream sugar and margarine.
3. Sift flour, baking powder and chick pea flour together.
4. Combine all ingredients and mix into a soft dough.
5. Remove a handful of dough and set aside. Take the rest of the dough and press it evenly in a tart tray (9 inches in diameter). Line tray with dough raising the edges up along the sides.
6. Spoon some jam into the base of the tart. Grate the dough which was set aside onto the tart. Cover jam evenly.
7. Bake on centre shelf of oven for 20 min or until crust turns golden brown.
8. Cool before slicing.

Apple –Pear or any Fruit Tart

Use the above recipe. Instead of jam, prepare fruit filling by stewing :
2 cups cleaned and chopped fruit and 1 cup sugar

Method:
Heat fruit with sugar and bring to boil. Lower heat and simmer until water is reduced.
Cool and use instead of jam.

Tanie Reena's Cheese Tarts

Preparation time: 10 min
Baking time: 20 min
Makes: 24

Ingredients:
1 cup flour
1 cup cheddar cheese
1 cup butter
½ tsp salt
Apricot jam

Method:
1. Preheat oven to 180° C
2. Mix flour cheese and salt together.
3. Rub in butter to make a soft dough.
4. Roll out about 3 mm thick. Cut into rounds and place in greased patty pans.
5. Bake for 15 min until golden brown.
6. Remove from oven and using the back of a tsp press down centre of tart to make a dent.
7. Remove from pan when cool.
8. Fill the centre of each tart with apricot jam.

Cheese Puffs

Preparation time: 10 min
Baking time: 30 min
Makes: 18

Ingredients:
1 cup flour
1 cup grated cheddar cheese
½ tsp salt
1½ tsp baking powder
1 cup milk

Method:
1. Preheat oven to 200° C.
2. Sift flour and baking powder. Add cheese and mix.
3. Drop teaspoons full into greased patty pans.
4. Bake for 10 to 15 min in a hot oven.

Fruit Loaf

Preparation Time: 20 min
Baking Time: 1¼ hours
Makes: 1 loaf

Ingredients:
1 cup flour
½ cup softened butter
¾ cup sugar
1 tsp bicarbonate of soda
2 tsp mixed spice
1 tsp ground cinnamon
½ tsp ground nutmeg
½ cup currants
½ cup mixed candied peel
2 tbsp golden syrup
1¼ cup butter milk

Method:
1. Preheat oven to 108° C.
2. Double line a greased loaf tin.
3. Sift flour into a large mixing bowl.
4. Rub in butter until mixture resembles fine bread crumbs.
5. Add spices, sugar, bicarbonate of soda, currants and mixed peel. Mix well.
6. Combine butter milk and syrup and stir into fruit mixture.
7. Spoon into baking pan. Bake for 1¼ hours or until skewer comes out clean.
8. Remove from oven, cool for a few minutes and then turn out on a wire rack.

Eggless Fruit Cake

Preparation time: 20 min
Baking Time: 1 hr

Ingredients:
½ cup sugar
¼ cup butter
2 cups flour
1 cup mixed fruit
2 tsp mixed spice
½ cup golden syrup
1 cup yogurt
1 tsp bicarbonate of soda
3 tbsp warm water

Method:
1. Preheat oven to 160° C.
2. Cream sugar and butter.
3. Add golden syrup and then yogurt. Mix well.
4. Add flour fruit and spice. Mix well.
5. Dissolve bicarbonate of soda and water and add to mixture. Mix again.
6. Put into prepared baking pan and bake for 1 hr.
7. Cool completely before removing from pan.

Boiled Fruit Cake – Large

Preparation Time: 40 min
Baking Time: 2 hrs

Ingredients:
1 cup sugar
1 cup water
½ cup butter
1 cup currants
1 cup sultanas
½ cup seedless raisins
1 cup chopped dates
2 tbsp chopped citrus peel
1 tsp mixed spice
½ tsp salt
1 tsp bicarbonate of soda
2 cups cake flour
1 tsp baking powder
¼ tsp ground cinnamon
¼ tsp ground ginger
¼ cup white vinegar

Method:
1. Preheat oven to 150° C.
2. In a sauce pan combine sugar, water, butter, fruit, mixed spice and salt and bring to boil. Lower heat and cook for 25 min. Leave to cool, when cold add bicarbonate of soda and vinegar.
3. Sift flour spices and baking powder in a large mixing bowl and combine all ingredients together. Mix well.
4. Spoon into prepared baking pan and level the surface.
5. Bake for 1 to 1½ hrs till skewer comes clean.
6. Remove from oven, cool for a few minutes and then turn out on a wire rack to cool.

PASTRY

Quick Hot Water Pastry --- for Sausage Rolls etc

Ingredients:
500 g butter or margarine
3ml salt
250ml boiling water
500ml flour

Method:
1. Place butter or margarine in a mixing bowl. Cut butter into pieces using a knife.
2. Pour boiling water on it.
3. Stand for 1 min and then stir in flour and salt. Mix thoroughly using a knife.
4. Place bowl with mixture in a refrigerator until it hardens.
5. Turn out on a floured board, roll out once or twice. Keep in refrigerator until required.

Sour Cream Pastry

Ingredients:
500ml flour
250g butter
¼ tsp salt
300ml sour cream

Method:
1. Sift flour and salt into a basin.
2. Cut butter inside the flour, into thin strips.
3. Add cream, mix with hands to make a dough. Do not knead.
4. Place in cling film in a refrigerator until required.

Pita Bread

Preparation Time: 1 hr
Baking Time: 10 min
Makes 12 pita bread

Ingredients:
6 cups flour
1 tsp salt
4 tbsp sugar
¼ cup oil
1 packet (7g) instant yeast
2½ cups warm milk mixed with water

Method:
1. Blend flour, sugar, and salt.
2. Mix warm milk, oil and yeast together.
3. Make a well into the flour and pour milk mixture into it. Mix and make a dough. Knead well, cover and allow to rise.
4. When it is double the size knock it down again. Make a long roll and cut into 12 equal pieces.
5. Roll each into equal size round shapes and again allow to rise.
6. While pita bread is rising preheat oven to 200° C.
7. Place on greased baking trays and bake for about 6 min. Remove from oven and cool till required.

Puri

Preparation Time: 10 min.
Cooking time: 30 min
Serves: 6

Ingredients:
3 cups flour
1½ tsp baking powder
½ tsp salt
¼ cup ghee or oil
Milk to make a soft dough
Cooking oil for deep frying

Method:
1. Sift flour, baking powder and salt.
2. Rub oil into flour mixture until it looks like fine bread crumbs.
3. Use milk to make a soft dough.
4. Roll out on floured board.
5. Break into little balls. Roll each ball into a round shape.
6. Fry in deep oil until golden brown. Drain in colander.

Roti (Parata)

Preparation Time: 30 min
Cooking time: 30 min
Serves: 6

Ingredients:
3 cups flour
½ cup ghee mixed with oil
¼ cup oil
1 tsp salt
2 tbsp sugar
1½ cups boiling water
½ cup flour for sprinkling (dusting)

Method:
1. Combine flour sugar salt ¼ cup oil in a mixing bowl.
2. Pour boiling water into the flour stirring to mix all ingredients. Allow to cool. Use hands to make a soft dough. Knead well.
3. Roll out on a floured surface into a large thin oblong shape. Brush surface generously with ghee and oil mixture. Sprinkle flour over the oil. Starting from the long side, roll the dough into a long Swiss roll.
4. Cut into 6 equal size pieces. Make into round balls, roll flat, as thin as possible.
5. Cook on a griddle pan or tawa (roti cooker). Brush with ghee mixture on either side. Cook until brown spots appear on both sides.
6. Serve with curried foods.

Milk Bread

Preparation: 1 hr
Baking time: 20 min
Makes: 1 loaf

Ingredients:
4 cups flour
1 sachet (7g) instant yeast
2 tbsp butter, melted
¼ cup cooking oil
2 tbsp sugar
½ tsp salt
1½ cups milk

Method:
1. Sift together flour and salt.
2. In a small bowl mix together milk, yeast, oil and sugar.
3. While mixture is still warm, add to flour and make a dough. Knead well.
4. Grease sides of dish, cover and allow dough to rise in a warm place.
5. When dough is double the size, knead the dough again. Roll into a long shape and place on a greased baking tray. Cover and allow to rise again to double its size.
6. Preheat oven to 200° C.
7. Place tray on centre shelf of oven and bake till golden brown in colour.

Herb Bread

Add to above recipe
1 tbsp brown onion soup powder
1 tsp mixed dried herbs
¼ tsp freshly ground black pepper

Koeksisters -- Plaited

Ingredients:
300g cake flour
3 tsp baking powder
½ tsp salt
3 tbsp butter
¾ cup water
3 tsp lemon juice
Oil for frying
Syrup:
1kg sugar
500ml water
2 pieces of fresh ginger, cleaned
2 ml cream of tartar
Pinch of salt
Grated rind and juice of ½ lemon

Method:
1. Sift together flour, baking powder, and salt. Rub in the butter.
2. Mix together lemon juice and water and add to flour to make a dough .Knead the dough until small bubbles appear under the surface. Cover and allow to rise for 30 min.
3. Prepare syrup.
4. Roll dough into a long rectangular shape, about 10 mm thick. Cut into long 20 mm strips. Press the ends of 3 strips together, and plait tightly. Cut into 70mm length and press ends together.
5. Fry in hot oil until golden brown on both sides.
6. Dip into cold syrup while still very hot. Use a wire rack to drain syrup.

Syrup:
1. Dissolve sugar in water in a sauce pan stirring all the time.
2. Heat while stirring until all sugar is dissolved.
3. Bring to boil. Continue to boil for about 5 to 6 min.
4. Remove from heat and cool. For rapid cooling stand in the refrigerator.

Larwa or Luddo

Ingredients:
Syrup:
2 cups sugar
1 cup water
¼ bottle egg yellow food colouring

Luddo:
1 cup gram (chick pea) flour
1½ tsp baking powder
1 tbsp ghee
¾ cup water
½ cup tinted slivered almonds
Oil for deep frying

Method:
1. Make a sticky syrup with sugar and water. Add colouring and set aside. Keep warm.
2. Sift dry ingredients and rub in ghee. Add water and make a thick batter
3. Heat oil. Pass batter through a colander or larwa press, into oil and fry till golden brown.
4. Using a slotted spoon remove the worm, like 'boondias' from the oil and steep immediately into the syrup.
5. The syrup will be immediately absorbed into the cooked batter. Remove from syrup and drain in a colander.
6. Repeat the process until all the batter is done.
7. Mould a handful into a ball, roll into coloured almonds and allow to dry. Complete moulding all the soaked batter. These balls are your luddo.

Gulab Jamun

Ingredients:
1 tin (397g) condensed milk
1 tbsp ghee
2½ cups flour
3 tsp baking powder
1 tsp cardamom powder
½ tsp bicarbonate of soda
Oil for frying
Syrup:
3 cups sugar
1½ cups sugar

Method:
1. Prepare syrup by combining sugar with water. Stir and dissolve sugar before heating. Bring to boil and lower heat. Boil until syrup thickens. Set aside and allow to cool.
2. Pour condensed milk into a mixing bowl. Add ghee and cardamom.
3. Sift together flour, baking powder and bicarbonate of soda and add to condensed milk mixture. Make soft dough.
4. Break dough onto small balls and roll into finger shapes. Do that with all the dough.
5. Fry a batch at a time till golden brown.
6. Remove from oil and dunk into syrup immediately.
7. Remove from syrup in a tray to drain on a wire rack.

Chana Magaj

Ingredients:
500g chickpea flour (chana flour)
60g powdered milk
2 tbsp ghee
500g icing sugar
500g butter
¼ cup milk
1 tsp cardamom powder
¼ cup coloured almonds

Method:
1. Combine chick pea flour and milk powder. Sprinkle milk and ghee on the flour and rub mixture to resemble fine bread crumbs. Allow to stand and dry for 1 hr.
2. Heat butter in a heavy based pan and fry the chana flour on medium heat, stirring all the time, till colour changes to light brown. You will smell the lovely aroma.
3. Add the icing sugar and cardamom powder and stir. Remove from heat and stir until well blended.
4. Pack into a deep tray very compactly. Smooth the surface. Sprinkle coloured almonds evenly. Press almonds down onto the fudge like surface.
5. Cool and divide into squares.

Burfee

Ingredients:
500g Nespray or Klim powdered milk
I small tin condensed cream
1 tbsp ghee
2 tbsp ground almonds
¾ cup sugar
1 tsp cardamom

Method:
1. Mix milk powder, almond powder, ghee and cream .Rub together till mixture is well blended.
2. In a sauce pan boil water and sugar, till syrup becomes sticky.
3. Pour into milk powder mixture and stir, till well blended.
4. Spoon into greased tray. Sprinkle coloured almonds evenly on surface and allow to cool and set.
5. Cut into squares.

Mini Dosa

Ingredients:
1½ cups urad flour (black lentil flour)
½ tsp bicarbonate of soda (baking soda)
1 tsp cumin powder
½ cup chopped fresh coriander leaves
¼ cup chopped onion
1 tsp finely chopped green chillies
1 tsp salt
Water to make a paste
Oil for frying

Method:
1. Mix all ingredients together. Add water to make a runny paste, like a pancake batter.
2. Use one tbsp oil to coat a nonstick pan .Put 2 tbsp batter in the centre of the pan and with quick movements spread into a circle using the base of the spoon to move the batter away from the centre.
3. The pan cake cooks quickly. Ease off the bottom and turn over.
4. Remove from pan and finish the rest of the batter.
5. Using a filling of choice wrap and serve while still warm.

Cous Cous Salad

Ingredients:
2 cups cous cous
¼ cup chopped sundried tomatoes
½ cup boiled mung beans
½ cup boiled masoor (brown lentils)
½ cup chopped nuts (pecan, cashew and almonds)
1 tbsp sesame seeds
1 tsp salt
¼ cup finely chopped onion
¼ cup chopped mixed herbs (parsley, coriander and chives)
Juice and rind of 1 lime or lemon
½ tsp freshly ground black pepper
2 tbsp olive oil

Method:
1. Prepare cous cous by pouring 2 cups of boiling water over it. Allow to soak and cool.
2. Mix all other ingredients together. Combine with cous cous and place in a serving bowl.
3. Serve immediately.

NB:
One can add chopped celery, green, red and yellow peppers etc…according to preference.

Vegetarian Mousaka ---Greek Style

Preparation time: 30 min
Cooking time: 60 min
Serves: 6

Ingredients:
100g butter
3 tbsp oil
2 brinjals, sliced and sprinkled with salt
4 potatoes, peeled and sliced into rounds, very thin slices
2 onions chopped
3 tomatoes skinned and sliced
1 tsp crushed garlic
1 can of beans of choice
1 tsp mixed herbs
1 tsp dried basil
Salt and pepper

Sauce:
3 tbsp butter
3 tbsp flour
2½ cups milk
250g grated cheddar cheese
1 tsp salt
½ tsp thyme
½ tsp freshly grated black pepper

Method:
1. In a saucepan heat butter and fry brinjal for 5 min and potatoes for 5 min.Remove and set aside.
2. Into the sauce pan add oil and sauté the onions. Add tomatoes, garlic salt and pepper and herbs. Add beans and cook for 5 min.
3. In another sauce pan melt butter for sauce. Add flour and cook till flour turns light brown stirring all the time.
4. Gradually add milk, thyme, salt and pepper. Cook till sauce thickens. Cool and add ½ the cheese. Set aside.
5. In a casserole dish, layer 1/3 of cooked vegetables at base. Top with 1/3 of sauce. Continue with layering ending with the sauce .Sprinkle with remaining cheese.
6. Bake at 180°C for 1 hour until vegetables are soft.
7. Garnish with parsley and serve with crusty bread.

Maizena and Mango Pickle

Ingredients:
2 dozen green mangoes
½ cup salt
½ cup mango pickle masala
2 tbsp chopped green chillies
3 tbsp crushed garlic
1 tsp chilli powder
1 tbsp cumin seeds
1 cup oil
1 tsp mustard seeds
Few sprigs of curry leaves

Paste:
1 cup vinegar
4 tbsp sugar
½ cup maizena

Method:
1. Peel mango, cut into slices and throw away seeds. Put into a bowl and cover with ½ cup salt. Allow to stand for 24 hrs. Mix every now and then.
2. Rinse mango and dry on kitchen towel. Add to the mango, the methi pickle masala, green chillies, garlic, chilli powder, and cumin seeds and mix well.
3. In a sauce pan make a paste of vinegar sugar and maizena. Bring to boil and cook till paste thickens. Add to mangoes and mix.
4. In the 1 cup oil add mustard seeds and curry leaves .Heat till mustard seeds begin to pop. Pour hot oil on mango mixture and mix well. Allow to cool. Bottle and use when desired.

Mango and Mint Dressing

Ingredients:
1 ripe mango, skinned and flesh finely chopped
150g natural yogurt
2 tbsp chopped fresh mint leaves
3 spring onions finely chopped
2 tbsp chopped coriander leaves
2 cloves garlic, crushed
1 green chilli, finely chopped
½ tsp salt
½ tsp freshly ground black pepper
3 tbsp olive oil

Method:
Mix all ingredients and serve with soya prawns or soya sausages

Curried Pineapple Salad

Preparation Time: 20 min
Cooking Time: 30 min

Ingredients:
2 large pineapples peeled and cubed
1 cup sugar
1 tsp salt
2 large onions sliced
1 tbsp crushed garlic
1 tsp chilli powder
1 tsp turmeric powder
1 tsp coriander powder
1 tsp cumin powder
1 pieces cinnamon sticks
1 tsp mustard powder
½ cup apple cider vinegar
2 tbsp corn flour

Method:
1. Combine all the ingredients except the corn flour into a sauce pan. Stir, cover and cook over low heat until sugar has dissolved. Bring to boil, lower heat and simmer for 30 min.
2. Add some water to the corn flour to make a paste and stir into the mixture.
3. Remove from heat and bottle in heated jars and seal.

Mango Salsa

Ingredients:
1 mango, chopped fine
1 green chilli, chopped fine
1 clove garlic crushed
3 tbsp finely chopped coriander
1 tbsp olive oil
½ tsp salt

Method:
Mix all ingredients and put into serving bowl. Serve as an accompaniment to soya prawns or stir fries or soya sausages.

Vegetarian Paella --- Spanish Style

Preparation Time: 45 min
Cooking Time: 30 min
Serves: 6

Ingredients:
250g diced carrots
250g peas
250g cleaned and diced potatoes
250g soya prawns
250 g soya chicken strips
1 large onion, chopped
2 cups rice
1 cup white wine
2 sticks cinnamon
4 cloves cardamom
4 cloves
1 tsp cumin seeds
1 tsp coarsely ground black pepper
1 tsp green chillies chopped
1 tomato deseeded and cubed
1 red, 1 yellow and 1 green pepper sliced and cut into cubes.
2 tbsp butter
½ cup olive oil
1 tbsp crushed garlic
1 tbsp freshly grated ginger
4 cups vegetable stock

Method:
1. Individually fry vegetables and soya products and set aside. Soya chunks have to be soaked in boiling water before frying.
2. Sauté onions in olive oil mixed in butter after adding cumin seeds, cinnamon, cloves and cardamom.
3. When onions turn light brown add green chilli, salt, pepper, ginger and garlic .Add white wine, and cook for 5 min.
4. Add rice and fry rice in oil mixture for 5 min. Add all other ingredients and stir before adding stock.
5. Cook until the rice has absorbed all the liquid.
6. Serve hot with a salad or salsa.

Aloo Fry (Fried Potatoes)

Ingredients:
4 large potatoes, sliced round very thinly
1 tsp cumin seeds
1 tsp chilli powder
1 tsp turmeric powder
1 tsp coriander powder
1 tsp cumin powder
1 tsp freshly grated ginger
1 tsp crushed garlic
1 tsp salt
¼ cup cooking oil

Method:
1. Into a large non stick frying pan put oil and all ingredients except the potatoes and cook for 1 min.
2. Add potatoes and stir till all the potatoes are coated. Cover and cook on low heat till potatoes are cooked soft but not smashed. Use a flat spoon, every now and then to turn them around.
3. Serve with khudi and kitchree.

Tandoor Masala

Masala is the name given to a number of spices combined to give off a particular taste and aroma. A Tandoor is a clay oven. Not all of us have clay ovens but we can create tastes similar to those we desire .I found an easy recipe to use without much fuss about a perfect formula. Use equal quantities of turmeric powder. Chilli powder, coriander powder, cumin powder, turmeric powder, ground fresh ginger, crushed garlic and salt.

For Example:
For 1kg of soya products, vegetables or paneer I would use:
1 tbsp turmeric powder
1 tbsp chilli powder
1 tbsp cumin powder
1 tbsp coriander powder
1 tbsp ginger paste
1 tbsp garlic paste
1 tbsp salt
Add with ½ cup tomato paste and
1 cup yogurt and you have your marinade for:

1. Tandoori vegetables
2. Breyani
3. Masala, butter soya chicken

For flavour and aroma: Normally --- 'BROWN' spices are added to the oil with the onion.
These are: cardamom pods, cumin seeds, cinnamon, star anise and cloves.

Basic Method for any Curry

Sauté the onions in oil. Add cinnamon, cloves, cardamom pods and cumin seeds.
Make a paste using a little water with chilli powder, turmeric powder, coriander powder, cumin powder ginger and garlic. The water prevents the spices from burning. When spices are added to hot oil they burn, turning bitter and also change colour. Spices are supposed to cook in oil, not burn.
Garam Masala is added at the end to add more 'heat'. These are toasted brown spices like cloves, coriander powder, cumin powder, black pepper and cinnamon.
Tomato and yogurt are tenderisers.
Food is best cooked on low heat.

REFRESHING DRINKS

Lassi -- Yogurt drink

Ingredients:
1 large mango peeled and flesh chopped
1 litre sour milk or yogurt
2 tbsp honey

Method:
1. In a food processor, process all ingredients till smooth.
2. Add water if consistency too thick.
3. Pour into tall glasses and serve as a refreshing drink.

Falooda and Bombay Crush

Ingredients:
½ packet falooda (agar agar) powder
1 litre water
½ cup sugar
1 tsp red food colouring
½ tsp cardamom powder

Method:
1. Boil all ingredients together until sugar dissolves. Falooda powder does not need a refrigerator to set.
2. Pour into one large serving bowl or into small individual bowls.
3. Serve as jelly.

Bombay Crush

Ingredients:
1 cup grated prepared falooda (as above)
2 tbsp subja seeds
½ cup boiling water
1 litre cold milk
4 tbsp rose syrup
Some ice cream or sorbet, if preferred

Method:
1. Pour boiling water onto subja seeds. Allow to stand and cool. The subja seeds will swell and become transparent.
2. Mix all ingredients into milk, stir and chill and serve in tall glasses.
3. If preferred leave out ice cream, top on milk just before serving.

Lemongrass and Rooibos Iced Tea

Ingredients:
4 stalks lemon grass, chopped
1 tbsp grated ginger
1 vanilla pod, chopped or
1 tsp vanilla essence
1 cup sugar
2 litres water
¼ cup lemon juice
Zest of 1 lemon
5 Rooibos tea bags
Lemon slices and mint leaves for garnishing

Method:
1. Combine all the ingredients in a large bowl. Pour boiling water over them and allow to steep for about an hour.
2. Stir well for sugar to dissolve.
3. Strain and refrigerate.
4. Add more water if too sweet.
5. Serve over ice cubes.
6. Garnish with a slice of lemon and fresh mint leaves.

Lemonade

Ingredients:
1 dozen lemons or lime
2 cups sugar
Some mint leaves

Method:
1. Use a grater and remove the zest of all the lemons. Set aside.
2. Squeeze the juice of all the lemons.
3. There should be about 2 cups of lemon juice.
4. Mix together lemon juice sugar and zest until all the sugar is dissolved.
5. Put the ingredients into a pot and boil for 5min. Allow to cool, strain and refrigerate.
6. Dilute if necessary. Serve over ice in tall glasses. Garnish with mint leaves.

Made in United States
Orlando, FL
01 December 2021

11026324R00084